Praise for *Start Your Business*

D0516780

'This is just what people toying with the idea of st[art]
to hear...the weekly format does help to break the
business into manageable chunks.'

The Sunday Times

"*Start Your Business Week by Week* is written in such a clear and friendly
way that you can't help being drawn into the excitement of becoming an
entrepreneur. Breaking down the process into weekly steps makes it
suddenly seem more achievable, and I'm sure many more people will be
encouraged to turn their ideas into their own businesses as a result."

Former Prime Minister Tony Blair

**A survey of readers found that 87% rated *Start Your Business Week
by Week* as 'Essential reading for start-ups'. Here are some of the
comments from these readers:**

'I bought your book yesterday and read it in one go last night. I have been
thinking about launching a business for the last year or so and now with your
help I feel I can do it. The structure is great, and the simple realisation that
starting a business is a process rather than an action was worth the cover price
alone.'

'I began seriously thinking about starting up again after two years away from
business. Working for someone else just isn't the same! I made several glaring
mistakes the first time around, and have found reading the book and using the
site a huge help in making sure the same mistakes won't be repeated.'

"I have been skipping merrily along through the weeks in my nifty business
book. Although I have read all the way through to Week Eight, I am still doing
business back in Week Three. Wherever I go, I tote my trusty notebook of ideas
plus my ever-increasing list of things to do!"

"I shall be recommending it to my 'cultural entrepreneurship' students at the
University of Warwick where I lecture and following the steps as I start up my
own business over the forthcoming 6–12 months."

'The magic words "Week by Week" on the front cover leapt out at me and I
thought "thank God someone's had the intelligence to write down how to start
up businesses in recipe style: WONDERFUL! It makes so much sense." The
book is written in a very accessible way: the content is well organised; it's full
of useful de-mystifying information, and is nicely peppered with
stories and anecdotes to keep you going through the darker hours. It is going
to have a heavy hand in making my idea come to life.'

Many more stories of businesses that started up using this book are
available on the website – and I'd love to hear your story too. Simply go to
www.weekbyweek.net/startyourbusiness

Steve Parks

Start Your Business
Week by Week

How to plan and launch your successful business –
one step at a time

Second edition

PEARSON

Harlow, England • London • New York • Boston • San Francisco • Toronto • Sydney
Auckland • Singapore • Hong Kong • Tokyo • Seoul • Taipei • New Delhi
Cape Town • São Paulo • Mexico City • Madrid • Amsterdam • Munich • Paris • Milan

PEARSON EDUCATION LIMITED
Edinburgh Gate
Harlow CM20 2JE
United Kingdom
Tel: +44 (0)1279 623623
Web: www.pearson.com/uk

First published 2005 (print)
Second edition published 2013 (print and electronic)

ISBN: 978-0-273-76866-1 (print)
       978-0-273-76992-7 (PDF)
       978-0-273-76993-4 (ePub)

British Library Cataloguing-in-Publication Data
A catalogue record for the print edition is available from the British Library

Library of Congress Cataloging-in-Publication Data
Parks, Steve, 1973–
  Start your business week by week : how to plan and launch your successful business--one step at a time / Steve Parks. -- 2nd ed.
      p. cm.
  Includes index.
  ISBN 978-0-273-76866-1 (pbk.) -- ISBN 978-0-273-76992-7 (PDF) -- ISBN 978-0-273-76993-4 (ePub) 1. New business enterprises. 2. Small business--Management. I. Title.
  HD62.5.P375 2013
  658.1'1--dc23
                            2012044307

10 9 8 7 6 5 4 3 2 1
17 16 15 14 13

Cover design by Nick Redeyoff
Print edition typeset in 11/14pt Minion Pro by 30
Print edition printed by Ashford Colour Press Ltd, Gosport
NOTE THAT ANY PAGE CROSS REFERENCES REFER TO THE PRINT EDITION

For all those brave enough to free their dreams from their heads and work hard, staying true to their values, to make them reality.

Contents

Acknowledgements

Firstly I'd like to thank everybody I've ever worked with since I started my first business at the age of 25. Those who have invested in my ideas, those who have worked with me to make them happen, and those who have provided advice and assistance along the way.

Special thanks to all 140 staff, and co-founders, at my current business, which is the most energetic and inspiring place I've ever worked.

Thanks to my parents for not going too mad when I ran my own pirate radio station, dropped out of university to take a job at the BBC, or left a safe and steady career at the BBC to start my own business. Thanks to my Dad for starting my fascination with business by taking me to his work from time to time when I was young and also by talking to me about his job, and thanks to Mum for teaching me how to research and learn for myself – rather than the school's method of simply cramming in what you needed to know to pass exams.

In an exception to the world of education in general I want to thank my primary school teachers at Doddington School in Kent (now closed down as a result of cutbacks, sadly), who gave me the encouragement and extra time in lessons that I needed to write my first book, *The Secret Trail*, at the age of nine. Thanks also to Young Enterprise, the organisation that allows young people to have a go at running their own real business. It was an eye-opening opportunity, and showed that running a business can be a real career choice.

And thanks too to Rebecca, Isabel and Alex for giving me the peace and space to finish this second edition in their lovely home in Tuscany – as well as good food and fun adventures between the writing.

Thanks to everyone at Pearson for being so great to work with – particularly Elie Williams, Rachael Stock and Richard Stagg.

And finally – thanks to you and all the other entrepreneurs who have read my books and got involved at the website. It's so rewarding to hear about your ideas turning into successful businesses.

About the author

Steve Parks began his career as a BBC radio journalist before launching his first business – an independent production company – at the age of 25.

In the last fourteen years he's experienced first-hand all that running your own business has to offer – from failures to successes.

Now 39, he's one of the co-founders of a web consultancy that has 140 staff and offices in nine countries. The company works for some of Europe's largest brands, as well as the public sector.

As well as building businesses, Steve writes and speaks about entrepreneurship, and outside of work he's a foodie. He lives in London, but looks forward to returning to the countryside.

Introduction

So, you're thinking of starting your own business? Congratulations: that makes you one of the most important people in the country. Entrepreneurs create jobs, provide innovative products and services, and serve local communities. They make things better.

Starting a business is one of the most challenging and rewarding things you can do in your life. It may surprise you, however, that only a select group of people ever try it. Statistically, if there are 1,000 people in the company you work in now, there are 390 who think they see an opportunity for a business.[1] Out of those how many will actually have a go at running their own business? Fifty, sixty? Nope. Statistically, three of you will become entrepreneurs.[2]

This number is so low because people are daunted by the prospect of running their own business. They think it's only for certain types of people, and they're not one of those types. They think it takes luck, or the right parents, or the right kind of education. Rubbish. But most of all they think it's too risky.

But the greatest rewards can only be achieved by taking action, and taking a risk.

The key is to accept that risk, and seek to manage it down to be as controlled as possible, rather than simply avoiding it in the first place.

The best way to do that is learning from entrepreneurs who have taken this journey before you, and that's what I've gathered together in this book.

I'm a journalist by background and I've interviewed hundreds of entrepreneurs over the years and worked to pull common threads out of what I learned from them. I've also run my own businesses. One that didn't work, some that did okay, and one that's a big success. I've learned so much from all of those experiences, and included those lessons (the good and the bad) in my recommendations here.

[1] Statistics from the Global Entrepreneurship Monitor United Kingdom.

[2] Statistic from the Barclays Small Business Survey Start Ups and Closures.

So this book will save you quite a lot of time and frustration, but you are still going to need to work very hard, particularly if you currently have a day job as well. You'll be working evenings and weekends. When your friends are off to the pub you'll be settling down to an evening of business. It will be hard to stick at it, but you are investing your time now for the future. In five years' time they will still be working Monday to Friday, nine to five, with only four weeks' holiday. They will still be earning similar-sized salaries. They still won't be able to get managers to listen to their ideas. Their lives will always stay the same, while you'll be taking charge of your life to shape it how you want it.

If you can work hard with self discipline,

and believe in yourself and your idea when other people doubt you.

If you can negotiate and deal with integrity,

and persevere when it would be so much easier to give up.

If you can do all this and more, while having fun, then your dreams are in reach

And what is more, you'll be an entrepreneur my friend. (Many apologies to Rudyard Kipling.)

Finally, I have a friend called Michel St-Onge in Canada who really is a rocket scientist. He has been through this book and says, 'It's not rocket science.' So relax, there'll be nothing you can't handle.

The Second Edition

So much has changed since I wrote the first edition of this book in 2004. The web has grown massively and become a part of everyday life – bringing some fantastic tools and opportunities for entrepreneurs. It's now cheaper and easier than ever to get a business up and running. But the long double-dip recession that started in 2008 shows no signs of recovering even now, and that's making financing a small business tricky – as well as making customers tighter with their money. On top of that, the entire business support network has been largely dismantled, and what remains has been reshaped.

It's a period of massive change for small business – but for entrepreneurs, everything is an opportunity – so I've taken the opportunity to largely rewrite this book. It's still a straightforward plain-speaking guide to getting a business off the ground in six months, but it's tailored for the new world of work we find ourselves in. I've focused on showing you how to build a business in a planned and methodical way with as low a financial outlay as possible.

I've also learned a huge amount in the meantime from running my own businesses, and have been able to refine a lot of the original ideas as a result.

This means that this second edition is very different from the first, and is a true guide to what's involved in starting a business now.

How to use this book

This book has been designed for people who are already employed but are looking to start their own business. Each chapter is a week's worth of work for this kind of person, and the whole process will take six months.

If you're not in another job at the moment you can probably complete each stage in two solid days, although you may still have to wait for other people, such as banks, accountants, HMRC and so on, to respond to your enquiries.

On the other hand you may be really busy and working long hours in your day job and need to do each chapter over a two-week period, starting your business in a year. It's up to you what speed you go at.

Within each week there are the following sections:

- **Shared Experiences**. Successful entrepreneurs explain what they did at this stage in their business and the lessons they learned, and entrepreneurs who have only just been through starting their company share their experiences.

- **To Do List**. Lists the jobs that need to be done this week, with some explanation of how to do them.

- **Recommended Reading**. This section lists other books that would be useful to read to get more detailed advice or inspiration on a particular subject relevant to the week.

- **List of Contacts**. This section lists the phone numbers, addresses or email addresses for people you need to contact this week.

- **Glossary**. Where necessary, this explains the meaning of words that you need to know about this week that you may not be familiar with already, such as financial jargon or a legal term.

Each week also includes a detailed explanation of what you'll be doing that week, why it's important, and how to do it.

I suggest you run your weeks to start on a Sunday, then you can start each week by reading the chapter thoroughly, and preparing for the week ahead. During the weekday evenings you can carry out most of the tasks, then have Saturday to round everything up and finish off – and maybe have time for a drink!

Meet Emma

To show you how the ideas in this book can be used in starting your company we're going to follow the progress of a fictional entrepreneur, Emma, through starting her business.

Emma is 27, and lives in Leeds. After graduating from university in the city (she's originally from a small village in Cornwall) she stayed and got a well-paid job in marketing for a financial services company. She's had two promotions since then, but has been getting bored. She never actually meets a customer, she doesn't find the product very exciting, and she doesn't get the opportunity to try any of her ideas. It's a big company and the emphasis is on keeping your head down and doing just the basic job. In her spare time Emma loves cooking good food and eating out.

Each Friday night Emma meets some of her old university friends for drinks in a local bar. Recently, as she's been getting more and more disenchanted by her job, they've been encouraging her to leave and start her own business.

You'll read about what Emma is doing at key stages throughout this book, but you can follow every single step of her journey on the website, including the documents she has to fill in, the letters she receives and sends, and the To Do lists she makes. You should feel free to adapt any of her letters, documents or lists for use in your own business.

The Website

There's a website to support this book at **www.weekbyweek.net/startyourbusiness** where you can read more about each of the stages, and ask questions.

One of the features on the website allows you to keep a diary, or blog, of your progress while starting your business. Once you've made it, it's fantastic to look back at all the ups and downs you experienced in the early days, the key decisions you made that contributed to your success, and to laugh at some of the mistakes you made. It's also great to read the blogs of other entrepreneurs to learn from people with the same kind of ambition as you.

This is not the law

Everyone is different and the aim of this book is not to make you conform to some set of rules to start your business. There's no 'secret formula'. This book is simply a guide, based on the experiences of a range of entrepreneurs and advisers, as well as my own experiences. You don't have to do everything it says in the order it's written. You can go off on tangents, do things in a different order, take longer to do some weeks, or shorter to do others, or just not do some things at all, and your business could still be a huge success. That's the beauty of being an entrepreneur – doing it your way.

This book is designed to be a guide, a reference suitable for busy people to enable them to concentrate on the more creative aspects of their business. It gives you contact details, website addresses, suggests good products and services to use, and provides other useful resources so that you don't have to spend the time finding them yourself – you can concentrate on starting your business.

A few warnings before you start...

A word on 'get rich quick'

There is no such thing as free money. Ignore the countless schemes that offer you an easy income. They generally give you a small slice of the action in return for you annoying all your friends by signing them up to the stupid scheme and selling them products they didn't really want but bought because you're their friend.

You'll gain nothing except more free time by doing this, and you'll get that because people will stop asking you out because they know you'll try to sell them something. Keep your friends. Don't bother with these schemes. Real wealth comes from hard work and good ideas of your own. Entrepreneurs know that profit is what you get as a reward for effort, creativity and risk. There are no shortcuts with a happy ending.

Also, one of the most surprising facts that I have learned about successful entrepreneurs from interviewing so many of them is that they don't do it for the money. They are motivated by a personal ambition, an absolute fixation on solving a particular problem, or just doing something to prove they can.

A word on integrity

There are entrepreneurs who have made money by doing dodgy deals or taking advantage of other people, but they nearly always meet an unhappy end. This could be because they get found out, or just simply because they have to live with the knowledge that they don't really deserve their money.

The only really happy millionaires I know earned their money honestly and with absolute integrity. Again, there are no shortcuts with a happy end.

Your rewards will be all the more satisfying if you have been ethical in your approach to starting your business. This means not taking advantage of your current employer by using work time or facilities for your private business. When you are the boss you'll be so disappointed if one of your staff were to take advantage of company time and resources in order to search for a new job or start their own business. Besides, it's always best to leave your job with them sorry to see you go, rather than celebrating your departure.

A word on 'red tape' and other excuses for business problems

As you're working on starting your business you'll read about the problems of government 'red tape' in the press. You'll hear people make speeches against it, and you'll see campaigns against it. These people say that 'red tape' (rules and regulations set by government) is causing huge problems for entrepreneurs in the UK.

My view on that has been reworded by my editor to be suitable for print, and now reads 'rubbish'. If you speak to any real, successful entrepreneur you'll find they've got more important things to focus on. They know that it's worth having a good accountant and a good lawyer to help them navigate through it. They know the value of expert advice that allows them to spend more time focusing on their main job – serving their customers and generating sales. And they know that if something is going wrong in their business, then they are responsible, not the government, not the EU, or anybody else.

The kinds of businesspeople who moan about 'red tape' are those in older, stagnant companies with older, stagnant management who are looking for someone else to blame for their problems. The same directors of those companies who spend the day moaning about the regulations they have to abide by will in their next breath be moaning about what's happened to their pension – and they'll say that the government should do something about it, there should be some kind of regulation to stop it happening!

In a civilised world there will always need to be rules and regulations, and in the UK they really are pretty reasonable – and this applies under governments of any political party. It's cheaper and easier to start a business in the UK than it is almost anywhere else – including in the USA, which is perceived as some kind of entrepreneurial Shangri-La!

You will come across many more important problems in starting your business than 'red tape'.

The message here is not to fall into the trap of blaming someone else for problems in your business. Real entrepreneurs know that 100 per cent of the responsibility for what happens to their business rests with them. No excuses.

Have fun

Starting a business will be one of the most exciting, challenging and rewarding things you have ever done. Enjoy it!

1 Week One:
The Beginning

Every great achievement starts in the smallest of ways. The essential first ingredient is the decision to start, to commit yourself. This week you'll be doing that and getting set up ready for the adventure ahead.

Time

More than money, it's time that's the most scarce and valuable commodity in building your business.

If you have a day job, you're lucky in many ways – you won't have to worry about money while doing your planning, but you will have to carefully plan your time. It's well worth blocking out particular evenings or weekends on your calendar to dedicate to your business – and you'll have to resist when friends invite you to the pub on those nights.

If you're not working at the moment, then money is perhaps going to be harder – but you'll have more time to devote to your business. If you can get some work, or do some freelancing, during the planning stage it'll take the pressure off a bit. But if you can afford to just focus on the business, or you don't have the option of getting a job, then you need to dedicate yourself to your work as if it is a proper job. Work hard every day. I've seen too many would-be entrepreneurs who never really made a go of their idea because they weren't strict enough about dedicating time to their business. They'd use the freedom they now felt they had to meet friends for lunch, run some errands, do some shopping and so on – and then be surprised each month when they hadn't made much progress.

To be your own boss, you need to be strict with yourself about working hard. Making your dreams reality takes dedication and hard work. While everyone else is playing, you'll be working to build your business – but it'll all be worth it in the end.

So, get your diary or your calendar and block out your work times for the next month, whether that's daytimes, evenings or weekends. Get into the habit of checking, reviewing and extending these bookings once a week.

If you don't already have a diary or calendar that you use, then that's the first thing for you to organise. It's up to you whether you want a cheap pocket diary, an expensive leather-bound organiser, or an electronic calendar on your smartphone or computer. It really depends on what works for you. The only advice I'd give is that spending more money doesn't make you more organised – so don't get carried away, and the fancy leather-bound organiser probably isn't necessary. Keep it simple.

Start getting into the habit of properly organising your time when you are working. I've recommended a book on p.9 called *Getting Things Done* which will really help you with this. Some quick tips that will help you manage your time are:

- Keep a list of all the projects you need to do, e.g. 'Open a bank account' (just an example, that task doesn't come up for a few weeks yet!).

- Write up the next action for each project, such as 'Pick up a business bank account pack from the local bank', and put this on your To Do list.

- Keep your To Do list prioritised. I used to write each task on an index card, and then I could sort the cards into order of priority easily. These days I use an app called Wunderlist that synchronises my lists across all my devices.

- At the end of each work session, review what you've done. If any tasks have been completed, what are the next actions that you need to write new tasks for? Plan your next work session by selecting the tasks you will do.

- Once a week have a full review. Do you need to add any new projects to your project list? Have all projects got a next action on your To Do list? Is your To Do list correctly prioritised?

As well as organising your time, it's important to recognise your efforts to stick to your plans. In the 'Recommended Reading' section on p.9 I include a link to a blog post about the method comedian Jerry Seinfeld uses to make himself write new material all the time. He takes a 'year at a view' calendar, puts it on the wall, and puts a big red cross through every day once he has written something. His mission is to 'never break the chain'. He wants every single day to have a big red cross, and he achieves it. That's what kept him motivated, and you can use the same trick. We're working through this book week by week, so take a week at a view calendar, and each week you can mark a cross, a big tick, a smiley face, or anything you like to show that you have read and done that week's chapter. Then you just have to make sure you don't break the chain. Starting things is easy, finishing them is hard, and this is one technique to help you be one of the people who gets to the end of this book having successfully started a business.

Workspace

If you're going to be working for yourself, you need somewhere to work. There are a range of options to choose from:

A proper office/shop/workshop. You really don't need to spend this kind of money just yet. Once you have your business plan and a clear budget you can look into this again. In the meantime you just need somewhere to work on your planning.

Co-working space. These are open-plan offices where lots of entre- preneurs and freelancers can all work. Often you pay a monthly membership fee which gives you a certain number of hours usage. Otherwise you may be able to just pay as you go. This is a luxury option because it gives you a clearly separate workspace, with added networking opportunities as a bonus. You'll be able to share experi- ences with other members and help each other out. If you can afford this, great. But don't spend money you can't afford – you can always move to somewhere like this later.

A home office. If you're lucky enough to have a spare room that you can turn into a home office, then this is ideal – dedicated space at a low cost.

The kitchen table. Plenty of very successful businesses have started from the kitchen table at home. It's slightly harder work because you have to keep clearing your things away, and you may get interruptions, but it's cheap and that counts for a lot at this stage. It's actually quite a nice place to work, and I often find myself working there, even though I have a nice home office! If you'll be working from the kitchen table or another space where you'll have to keep packing your work away, get a big box you can keep everything in somewhere nearby.

A café. There are plenty of cafés around that don't mind people lingering there, and many even offer free Wi-Fi. I'm actually writing this chapter in one!

Your local library. Most libraries now offer computer facilities and some quiet spaces to work and read. Many also offer Wi-Fi.

Of course, you can mix it up between these places to give yourself some variety – that's what I like to do.

This week, get your workspace ready, so that all the things you're likely to need are close by and you don't have to waste time popping out to get them. Notepads, sticky notes, lots of pens, envelopes, stamps, stapler, hole-punch, lever arch files and so on all come in useful. I also like having a big stack of index cards to plan things out on. More on that in a couple of weeks. But again, don't spend lots of money on this stuff and keep things minimal and simple.

Technology

It's technology that has made it so much easier to start and run a business than ever before, and throughout this book I'm going to give you lots of recommendations for websites and software to help you out.

It's really going to help if you have your own computer. It doesn't need to be a fancy one, just as long as you can access the internet. But if money is too tight right now you don't need to rush out and buy one.

At this stage it's wise to save money wherever you can. Instead you can use computers in internet cafés, libraries or some business support centres.

You're also likely to need a phone. For now you can just use your existing home phone or your mobile, and sort out a business line later only if it really becomes necessary.

It's worth having an email account for work. This is just temporary for now, as you don't know your brand name yet, but it'll be useful. If you already have one with a business suitable address (not sexything8000@ hotmail.com for example!) then it's fine to use that. But you can set one up quickly and for free at a number of mail services if you need to. I find Google's **Gmail.com** is the best mail provider because of the features they provide, and also they have really got the spam problem under control – plus, it's free!

In terms of other useful applications for use on your computer or smartphone, there are many available either as software to install on the computer or to use in a web browser. I'll mention some as we go, but to get you started, two of my favourites are:

Evernote. This is a really handy note-taking application. It makes it easy to store, organise and search all the ideas and research that you'll be doing. **www.evernote.com**

Google Reader. This allows you to subscribe to 'feeds' from websites, and gathers any new articles into one place. **www.google.com/reader**

Support and advice

The organisations that support small businesses in the UK have been going through a big shake-up in the last few years. As a result, a lot of the business support schemes have been cut, or are in flux – including Business Link. The official government business support website is now part of the main GOV.UK site at **https://www.gov.uk/browse/ business**. It isn't yet as comprehensive as the old Business Link site, but it is simpler to navigate. Fingers crossed they'll gradually make it more useful.

There are also various local projects. To get the latest information for where you are, I'd recommend doing a web search for some of the following phrases, with [place] replaced by your county, or your nearest town or city:

- Start-up business advice [place]

- Business support [place]

- Starting a business [place]

At this stage don't commit to any business support that requires a fee, equity (shares in your company) or any formal contract. There are plenty of useful free resources out there, and plenty of time for you to think about that kind of arrangement before you commit to it. Also, you don't need any professional advice such as a lawyer or accountant at this stage. That'll come later.

In terms of informal sources of support and advice, there are hundreds of useful and interesting books – and most of the successful entrepreneurs I know read them voraciously, devouring the ideas and experience inside. You'll find a list of books that I, and other readers of this book, have recommended, at **www.weekbyweek.net/startyourbusiness/reading** and I'll mention some of my particular favourites throughout this book. Use some of the time this week to pick your favourite selection of books and start reading them.

There are plenty of resources on the web. I'll mention useful websites as we go through each week, but as what's available on the internet changes so rapidly it's also worth checking my up-to-date recommendations at **www.weekbyweek.net/startyourbusiness/weblinks**. As part of getting started this week, browse through these websites.

There are also various clubs and events for start-ups. It's worth having a look on **www.meetup.com** for some. These are generally free (or very cheap) and you just meet in a café or bar for a drink and a chat. It's good to get to know others facing the same challenges as you.

Join the community

There's a great community on our website, with thousands of other people with similar dreams and ambitions. It can be tremendously motivating to know that you're not alone, and to help each other out along the way.

The website is at **www.weekbyweek.net/startyourbusiness**.

Join the community by registering on the site for free, and then make your first weekly blog post to write about what you found out this week in your research, what you achieved, and how you feel. This is not only good to let people know what you've done, and what problems you've encountered and need help with – it's also a great way of recording the history of your company. One day, when you're successful it'll be great to remind yourself how you got started.

Commitment

So, you've allocated time to set up your business, set up your work-space and technology, and investigated business support. You've also joined a community of people with the same kind of ambition.

These are the first small but essential steps on the road to making this happen. But you need one more thing.

In these 26 weeks there are going to be times when you feel a bit lost, times when you doubt you have what it takes, and times when you're on the verge of giving up.

Anything that is really worth achieving is hard work. The willingness to do that hard work and see the job through to the end is what makes people successful in any field – from athletics to business.

Make that commitment to yourself, and to your dream of building your own business. Commit to work hard, and to stick at it. Promise this to yourself.

Shared Experiences

Trenton Moss is the entrepreneur behind Webcredible, one of the UK's leading consultancies for website usability. His company now commands premium fees and counts Sony, eBay and ASDA among its clients, but Trenton started out as a one-man band like the rest of us:

'My first office was a desk on the landing of my shared, rented house. It was just outside the room of an amorous couple, who used to get quite annoyed if I was working too late at night. My only start-up costs were a cheap computer, a phone and a pencil case.'

THIS WEEK'S TO DO LIST

- ☐ Plan in working times for the next month.
- ☐ Identify where to work, and get it organised.
- ☐ Get a computer with internet access; or
- ☐ Find out where you can regularly access an internet-connected computer in the time you plan to work on the business.
- ☐ Set up a business-suitable email address.
- ☐ Research available business support and advice.
- ☐ Choose some useful and inspiring books.
- ☐ Browse websites about entrepreneurship.
- ☐ Register on the Week by Week website: **www.weekbyweek.net/ startyourbusiness**
- ☐ Write your Week One blog on the website.
- ☐ Mark off that you've completed this week on your calendar.

THIS WEEK'S RECOMMENDED READING

Getting Things Done, by David Allen (Piatkus).

This is a great book on how to make more effective use of your time. It provides realistic, simple and practical steps to take to be better organised. Time is the scarcest resource in a start-up business, so learning how to use it better is a worthwhile investment.

Jerry Seinfeld's Productivity Secret – a blog at lifehacker.com:

http://lifehacker.com/281626/jerry-seinfelds-productivity-secret

2 Week Two:
The Future

This week you'll work out the meaning of life, the universe and everything. And... well, actually that's enough for one week!

You have an idea to start a business and that's brilliant. Even better than that, you're obviously one of the few people who will take the next step and put their idea into action.

But let me stop you in your entrepreneurial tracks for just one week before we start you on the quest for world domination in your industry.

I know that for an entrepreneur this seems completely unnatural. Surely we should be picking up the phone and doing deals, going to meetings and selling things? Let's do, do, do! But there is a time for thinking too, and this is it.

The meaning of life

What is the meaning of life? For you as an individual, not mankind – we only have a week. Where do you want to be in five years, ten years or when you're old and grey? What will life look like and feel like? Where will you be? Who will you be with? What will your home be like? What will your financial status be? How will you spend your time? What will make you happy?

This week is about letting your mind roam free to find your dreams. Let's make sure that all the work you are going to put into starting your business is going to take you in the direction you really want to go.

You may already have had lots of dreams of the future, but this week you can really focus them, to get a clear vision of what you are aiming for.

Imagine the future

This week I want you to take every opportunity you can to daydream. I know you've been told off for that in the past at school or at work, but daydreaming is a really useful tool that's been used by many of the world's great thinkers to come up with amazing ideas and inventions.

Daydream in the shower, in the bath, while having breakfast, on the bus or train or in the car. Daydream during your lunch-break, while you're on hold or in a lift. There are lots of times during the day when you can let your mind wander for a few minutes.

The only restrictions are not to daydream during important meetings with your boss or in affectionate moments with your partner. It really doesn't go down well.

Be true to yourself

There's a tendency for people dreaming about the future to think of opulent surroundings – enormous houses on beautiful islands in the sun, a fleet of flashy cars, a yacht, expensive watches or jewellery and the most sophisticated parties attended by the powerful and the famous.

We've been kind of conditioned to believe that this is what success and happiness look like. In reality though, all that stuff doesn't make people happy.

The things that make people truly happy are simpler. People tend to be happy when:

- They and their family are safe and comfortable.

- They feel in control of their daily life and their destiny.

- They feel that what they do is valuable to others in some way.

- They are able to do things they are passionate about.

- They have a bigger goal they are working towards.

When I started my first business at the age of 25 I had dreams of big houses around the world, a flashy car, a lavish lifestyle and even owning a plane! Now I've had some more life experience, been to some successful entrepreneurs' big flashy houses and discovered more about myself, I've realised that I really don't want that at all. In reality my dream home is a small cottage in the English countryside with a fantastic kitchen and kitchen garden (I love to cook), in a village with a great pub, and with beautiful countryside in the area for hiking.

One of the earliest goals I set myself is the one that made me happiest when it was realised. The father of one of my closest childhood friends was a famous writer. I remember one time – I must have been about eight years old – we went into his study, and one of the bookshelves was full of copies of books he'd written. Not just in English, but in the many languages they had been translated into around the world. I vowed that one day I would have a bookshelf just like that with my books. I set about writing my first novel which I finished when I was nine, and it ran to over 100 pages. I got two gold stars at school and was immensely proud of my achievement! Imagine how it made me feel when, just over twenty years later, the publisher sent me the first copies of the first edition of this book – and then translated copies of it would arrive from time to time over the next few years, gradually filling up my bookshelf. That satisfaction had nothing to do with money (which is very lucky, because being a business book author is not a route to riches!). It was about achieving a big goal – that very clear picture in my mind of the bookcase with my books on.

So it's important to think about what actually matters to you, and be true to yourself in imagining the future, rather than just trying to conform to what the media portrays as the results of success.

The daydream

Picture this: it's a morning exactly twenty years from now. That's such a long time in the future that you can let your imagination run wild.

You wake up in your home, stretch, and look around you.

Where is your home in the world? What does the room look like? Is there anyone in the bed with you? Who? What are they like (as a person, not in bed!)? What is the weather like outside the window? What time is it? Who else is in the house? Children? Visiting friends?

After a while you get out of bed, go for a shower, and start your day. In your mind, picture every room in your house as you go through it. Get really specific. Imagine the size of the room, the colour scheme, the type of floor, the windows, the furniture in the room. The more specific you are, the better.

Often people have one or perhaps two rooms in their dream house that are really important to them. What are yours? A gym? A study? An amazing kitchen? A peaceful library? A swimming pool? A beautiful and relaxing bedroom?

Follow your morning routine now. What do you do? Where do you go?

Do you leave the house? When? Where do you go? Do you go by car, foot or public transport? Imagine that in detail.

If you're going to spend today on leisure, is that sport? Family time? Socialising? A hobby? Imagine the activity in detail. Where do you go, what does it look like? How do you feel? How do others around you feel?

If you're going to work today, do you work from home or travel to a workplace? What work do you do? Where? How do you get there? What time do you get there? What happens when you arrive? What does it look like? What do you do there? Who works with you? Again, imagine every room in your workplace as you did with your home.

Follow through your day. What do you do at each stage? At the end of your day, what next? Social life? Who with? Where? Doing what?

If this has covered a weekday, try also daydreaming about a weekend day, and vice versa.

So many questions! The questions above are designed just to start you thinking. After that you can let your mind roam wherever it goes. You don't have to answer each question, just watch the pictures that appear naturally in your mind.

If you're not used to daydreaming, it does get easier and more natural with practice. Don't worry if it doesn't feel right at first, just keep at it. Trust me.

I can't stress too often how important the detail is. See the pictures in your head as if you're watching a film. See the colours, the space, the light. Hear all the sounds, the conversations. And, just like the BBC, don't be scared of repeats. You can dream the same daydream again and again all week, adding more detail each time.

If you have a husband/wife/partner, then it's important to involve them in this process and imagine your life together in the future. You don't want to be dreaming of living six months of the year in sunny Australia if all they want from life is to live on a remote Scottish island. You'll need to talk your dreams over and decide on what you both want. Your partner will also be providing you with a huge amount of support and understanding while you put a lot of hard work into your business, so it's important that you share the dream.

Bring it closer

So, you've imagined life in twenty years' time. Now try imagining it in ten years, and even five years.

Turning mind pictures into real pictures

In the next six months, as you build your business, it's important to be reminded of what you're aiming for long term. To help with that I really recommend having a real or virtual pinboard on which you can put up photos and other things that will evoke your dreams.

For a real pinboard you can just get a simple cork noticeboard from a stationers, or stick pictures directly on a wall.

For a virtual noticeboard, you could use Evernote (which I mentioned last week), or otherwise I recommend **Pinterest.com** – once signed up you can add a button to your browser, and then search around the web for pictures of what you want. Then simply click the button to add any images you find to your Pinterest board. Emma registered at http://pinterest.com/emmacornish/ and created a 'future' board and also a 'mottos' board for inspirational mantras she wants to live by, and a food board because, well, she just loves food.

You can search for images on Google, or browse around websites or magazines for the subjects you're interested in. It's also worth browsing other people's boards on Pinterest to find inspiration.

If you do have a virtual board, it's still worth printing out some of the things that are particularly important to you and pinning them up near where you'll be working for that extra bit of motivation.

More than pictures

There are lots of other things you can put on your board too. Here are just a few:

- Write a cheque to yourself, dated five years from now. This is your pay cheque. How much will you be earning?

- Write some letters that you might receive in five years. Who will they be from? A member of staff at your company? An investor? A customer? The prime minister? A business hero of yours? Someone you or your business has helped through your work?

- Perhaps there will be some magazine or newspaper articles about you in five years? What will they say? If you don't have time to write a mock-up of these, just cut out a suitable real article and change the names!

- Photocopy your bank statement. Change the date, and change the balances! How good does that feel?

- Put a page from a calendar on the board. Change the date to a future one, years from now, and fill in the things you'll be doing on each day.

- You could even get models of some of the things you dream about – such as a car.

The point

Some of you will love all this. Others will think 'It's all a bit wishy-washy and pointless. When are we going to get onto the detailed stuff?'

There are two reasons why all this daydreaming and picturing the future is important, and why it's so important to actually put those pictures on your board.

First, you need to be sure that running your own business really is a part of your dreams for your future. It's best to find this out now rather than in two years' time when you've left your job, invested your money and time and put everything you have on the line – only to find out that you really dream of becoming a professional dry-stone waller in the Yorkshire Dales (that's not a random example, I've met someone who made that switch!).

The second reason is that we really do get what we focus on. If you have this picture of your future in your mind then it will open up all sorts of opportunities. Simply having a focus makes you more aware of people talking about things that can help you achieve this future. Those passing comments could be just the connection you need to make your business and your plans work. If you didn't have that focus they would just be passing comments.

I'm not just saying this because I vaguely believe it – I know it to be absolutely true because I've experienced it.

Making it happen

Now you know what your life will look like in five years. It's no longer just a dream – it's a plan. So how do you make it happen?

Start. It will always stay a plan unless you start something now that sets you on the road to achieving all of this. So for example if you've decided that you want to have your own plane in five years, you'd better start by subscribing to a magazine about learning to fly small aircraft. You might even buy a flight simulator program for your computer. You can learn the jargon, get into the community, then perhaps have a real flying lesson to try it out. As time goes on you can get more serious about it, taking enough lessons to get your pilot's licence and so on. But you have to start somewhere and you have to start now.

Get some symbols. If you want a Porsche in five years, do what Jonathan Elvidge did (see 'Shared Experiences', p.18) and start by having a model Porsche on your desk. You'll see it every day and remind yourself of what you're aiming for.

Talk to people. The more you tell people about your plan, the more opportunities will open up. If you've decided that you'll have a second home in the south of France, you might mention it to someone and find out that a friend of theirs has one already and would be happy for you to visit and find out what it's like, explore the area, and get to know the market. This stuff happens every day. Help it happen to you by letting people know what you're aiming for.

Re-visit your plan regularly. Once a month make some time in your diary to look at your plan again. Do you want to add, change or remove anything? Your plan will always evolve, so don't be scared of changing it. Is there anything you should start now? Any new symbol you could get? Anything you should be talking to people about?

To finish the week

At the end of this week you need to round up everything you've thought about. You might find that you've learned a lot about yourself. You'll certainly have a clearer picture of where you're going.

Have a meeting with yourself (and maybe your partner too) and review what your future holds. This meeting will really help you develop a clear focus and action plan out of all these dreams and ideas. Ask and answer these questions:

- Does what's on my pinboard reflect accurately what I've been daydreaming about?

- Of these dreams, what's going to be most important to me to achieve in the next five years?

- What do I need to do to achieve that, in terms of income, time, lifestyle etc.?

- Will starting my own business get me to where I want to be?

- Will I start a business? Yes or No.

- What else will I start doing now to achieve my plans in five years?

Shared Experiences

Jonathan Elvidge was the original founder of a retail chain called The Gadget Shop. It was tremendously successful until he sold majority control to outside investors. He's since set up a similar retail chain called Red5. He says:

'I was working for a telephone company as a technical sales adviser. I'd been dreaming of running my own business ever since I'd found it difficult to buy imaginative presents for people. Before I even left the phone company I'd built a balsa wood model of how my shop would look, decided what kind of car I would have when I was rich (a Porsche 911 in black) and bought a matchbox model of it to put on my desk at work, and I daydreamed about my lifestyle. I used my holidays to visit trade fairs around the world to look at and hold the products I wanted to sell. I ran the business and my future lifestyle in my head for months before I made the commitment to start it.'

Gary Klesch had a high-flying career in finance before becoming an entrepreneur – including a period working at the White House in the 1970s where he put together the finance for the Space Shuttle project. You would think money would be the thing to motivate him:

'I have always been driven by the intellectual challenge, I have never been driven by money – and nobody ever should be. If somebody is truly good, the money will follow, so focus on being good at something. People who focus on money mix up their priorities, and end up being dissatisfied.'

Steve McDermott is one of Europe's top motivational speakers (see p.19 for details of his book). He says:

'It has been proven beyond any doubt, in study after study, that high achievers have clearly defined what they want to do with their lives, and have lots and lots of reasons why they want to do it. They have a crystal clear vision of the future. Yet the fact remains that very few people give it any serious consideration. So few people achieve success, because so few people know what success they want.'

THIS WEEK'S TO DO LIST

☐ Daydream. A lot. Picture your life in the future.

☐ Create a real or virtual pinboard, filled with images of this future.

☐ Add other things to your pinboard that illustrate your life in five years. Letters, calendars, cheques, bank statements, magazine articles. Get really creative about this.

☐ Have a meeting with yourself at the end of the week, in front of your pinboard, to focus in on what you want and decide whether starting your own business is the route you want to take to get there.

THIS WEEK'S RECOMMENDED READING

How to be a Complete and Utter Failure in Life, Work and Everything, by Steve McDermott (Prentice Hall Business).

This is really entertaining, but the underlying message is serious and very inspiring. Steve has lots to say about the importance of setting your vision and goals.

3 Week Three:
Where Are You Now?

> This week you're going to review the time, money, expertise and contacts that you already have.

Before we start this week's activities, give yourself an honest answer to this question – did you actually do last week's activities, or have you just skipped through to this week?

'I've done them!'

Have a gold star, and then move on to the paragraph headed 'The current reality'.

'I didn't do last week's activities, I skipped ahead to this week.'

I know your type! I asked the question because I know how I would be with a book like this. I'd be so excited to get on with things and get my business going that I'd be skipping through the steps and ignoring anything that seemed either a bit airy-fairy or dull. I'm expecting some of you to be just like me – and you're going to be watched more closely than the rest!

The likelihood is that you have a very high entrepreneurial potential. You're a person who has lots of ideas, lacks patience, and just wants to do stuff. But you need to focus your energy and your passion with some clear thought in order to succeed, or you'll just end up going, very dynamically, in completely the wrong direction.

Trust me – do all the stuff suggested each week. Have fun doing Week Two this week, and we'll see you here again next week. It really will be easier to start your business this way.

The current reality

This week we're going to work out where you are now in your life in terms of the key resources you're going to need: finance, time, knowledge and contacts. These are all going to be highly important in starting your business.

Starting a new venture is very time consuming and you need to work out where that time is going to come from. And if you don't know anything or anyone connected with your chosen line of business, you'll need to invest some of that precious time to increase this knowledge before you take the leap.

We're also going to work out where you are financially, but don't worry if you're not loaded – there are other ways to raise the money you need to start your business.

This is where we first come across one of the key beliefs of entrepreneurs: the money follows. It's the result of everything else that happens, not the starting point. Soon you'll find that the money you need to start your business follows as a result of your ideas, your knowledge, your contacts and the time you invest. Do everything else right and the money comes to you.

Time

Is it a new week already?! Last week seemed to whizz by! Where does all the time go?

Much more than money, time is going to be your biggest challenge in starting your own business – finding the time to do everything that needs to be done. Time marches on while you're asleep, at the day job, on the train or bus or in the car, watching TV, eating, socialising and so on. Are you going to be able to find the time to make your business successful?

The likelihood is that you already have a job, and are reading this book to help you work out how to use what precious little 'spare' time you have in order to start your own business. You'll probably want to keep the day job while you go through the process of starting up, and it may be that your business is the kind that you can just run at evenings and weekends after that too.

In America it's far more common than here in the UK for people to 'moonlight' and run their own business while holding down a full-time job at the same time. Often this is just to test a business idea before they leave the comfort of a 'steady' job, which is a really sensible way to do things if you can.

This week you'll fill in a simple form estimating how you spend your time. This will give you an idea of where your time goes and how you can find time for your business.

Take a look at the weekly time sheet on p.32. Either copy one out for yourself or download the template from **www.weekbyweek.net/start yourbusiness/week3**, and fill in each of the squares with the activity you do at that time. You may want to do this day by day during the week, filling in what really happens, or you may want to do it all at once, estimating what you do each day. Either way is fine.

Work through the following list, but also add in everything else you do that isn't listed here:

- Bed. Fill in all the time you spend in bed, sleeping or pursuing other activities!

- Work. Fill in the time you spend at your day job.

- Travel. The time you spend getting to and from work. When else do you have to travel?

- Family. Do you have family commitments to children, parents, partners or other family members? Fill in a realistic assessment of the time you spend on this.

- Sport. Gym, football, squash, golf. If you do any of these, or other sports, block out this time.

- Hobbies. Do you go to dance lessons, do amateur dramatics, write, sing, spot trains or any other hobbies? I won't tease you about any weird hobbies, honest.

- Eating. Fill in your meal times.

- TV. Make this a separate category, so you can really see how much time you spend in front of the goggle box! This is where you might be able to reclaim a lot of time for your business.

- Socialising. Going to the pub, clubbing, visiting friends or going out to a restaurant.

- Housework. Again, add time spent on chores to the chart.

You'll start to see the grid become pretty full. So where are you going to find time for planning and starting your business?

Time-creating ideas

People sometimes ask how I manage to fit so much into my life – running a business, writing books, speaking at events, cooking, travelling and plenty of socialising. I'll share my secret with you – I have an extra two hours each day compared to the average person in the UK. That's 14 hours a week! Where does this time come from? I watch hardly any telly. By hardly any I mean about an hour a week on average. If there's a series I really like, then I'll either record it on the digital video recorder, or get the DVDs, and watch an episode when it suits me, not when the schedulers have decided I have to watch it.

Do you have a 'friend' who switches the telly on as soon as they get home? Or perhaps switches it on to watch a particular programme, but then it stays on with them flicking around the channels until bedtime? Would you like some advice for this 'friend' of yours? Cut out the telly and reclaim your – sorry their – life!

You don't have to cut it out altogether, but I bet a lot of the programmes you end up watching are ones you're not really bothered about. How about getting a copy of the *Radio Times* or the newspaper TV guides each week and going through it, circling the programmes that you *really* want to watch? Then you only switch on to watch these, and have the self-discipline to switch off again afterwards – or just record them as I do and watch them when you want a treat.

You'll be amazed at how much time you can claim back in this way. At the end of the day, do you want to achieve your dreams in life or spend a couple of hours a week watching misery on Albert Square?

OK, lecture over!

Here are some other ideas to create time for your business:

Set aside one full day each weekend and one or two evenings a week for your business. This should be enough time in the first six months. If this time is blocked out in your diary you can be more focused and more self-disciplined when the pub or the sofa beckons! This will also help avoid the other problem of your work spilling out across the whole week and annoying your partner! Of course if you don't have another job at the moment you'll be able to do your work in the working day and time will be less of a problem.

Do you have any holiday owing to you in your day job? Perhaps you could take a day off each month for the next six months and use that time for your business.

Do you have any evening or weekend activities that you do which you're not really passionate about? Perhaps you act as an official for a local club or society, or are simply a member. If you're going to start your own business you need to focus on that and tactfully leave previous commitments behind.

If you have children, perhaps you could have an arrangement with some friends where you look after their children as well as your own on a set night every other week, and they take care of all the children on the alternate weeks. That frees them for social activities once a fortnight and frees you to run your business one evening a fortnight.

Take a few minutes to plan time for your business over the next month and write it in your diary. Each week from now, plan in a further week's work on your business, so that you are always a month ahead. Once you have booked in this time for your business, stick to it.

Money

Before I say another word about money I want to say this: you don't need to be rich in order to start your own successful business.

It's certainly easier to start a business if you are rich, but having lots of money doesn't give you any advantage in terms of starting a *successful* business. You can spend a fortune on advertising, flashy offices or consultants – but if you don't get the basics right your business will still fail, however much you spend.

People start businesses all the time with very little or no money of their own. I started mine when I was still in debt with my student loan, and the monthly salary from the job I left had only been enough to cover my living costs. I had no savings or investments to cash in.

The money follows. Get your idea right, get your attitude right, work hard, and the money follows.

So, now we've dealt with that, it's time to find out exactly where you are financially. This is important because if you don't know now then you'll hit money problems later on.

Get together your recent bank statements, credit card statements, household bills, details of investments, your last month's till receipts and details of other income and expenditure and spend a few moments filling in a copy of the Personal Asset Statement and Monthly Budget worksheets on pp.33–35.

What's the result?

'I'm horribly in debt!'

OK, the next step is to get some advice. If you are in debt and finding the monthly repayments difficult then go and talk to your local Citizens Advice Bureau. Their opening hours are very difficult for anyone who has a job, and you can't book an appointment for a first visit, but bear in mind that they are all volunteers.

Once you've had some advice from them, it's also well worth speaking to the people you owe money to. You may be able to come to an arrangement with them. Do get advice on this though.

If you're mildly in debt you can probably work through it yourself, especially if you can easily afford the repayments. There are some useful websites with excellent advice on personal finance and getting out of debt. See the Week Three section of the website for details.

'I'm OK, but not in any way loaded.'

That's fine. Be aware of your monthly outgoings – and therefore how much you will need to keep earning if you give up the day job. We'll use this when it comes to planning your business later. It's a good idea if you can start saving some money now so that you will have some spare later. Cut back on a few luxuries and put the money in a savings account. Every pound you save now really will help later.

'I'm rich!'

Lucky you, that takes some of the worry away but you have just as much hard work ahead as everyone else!

Your credit report

While we're on the subject of finance, you should order a copy of your credit report now – even if you're really rich! This shows you exactly what the banks and other lenders will see when you apply to them later – the banks will check this even if you just want to open an account without borrowing any money. It's really important to know that there are no entries on your file that could damage your credit score with a bank. These could be incorrect or even fraudulent. If there are any, you can hopefully do something about it before you go to open your account.

There are three credit reference agencies which compile credit information in the UK: Experian, Equifax and Callcredit. You need to apply to each separately, and they have to provide you with a copy of your file (the 'statutory credit report') for a maximum fee of £2. Be careful though, because they will try to sell you more expensive reports and services. You only need the 'statutory' credit report, and they can make this very difficult to find on their websites – so do search around until you find it, and don't be upsold to more expensive ones. You'll find contact details for the agencies on p.30. If you write to them, give them your full name, date of birth, current address and any previous addresses you have lived at in the last six years, as well as any previous names you have been known by in that time.

Expert advice

Neil Ballantyne is a business bank manager. He says:

> 'I'd always advise people to check their credit record. On our compu-
> ter it just shows up as "adverse information" if there's a problem and
> we don't know whether it's a County Court Judgment for thousands of
> pounds, or a utility company that has been overzealous in chasing the
> £17 you owed at a house you moved out of three years ago. If you can
> show us your credit record and any supporting documents we can take
> a sympathetic and supporting view. We also see a surprising number
> of cases where people have incorrect information on their file that
> causes them problems. Get your credit record and sort it out.'

Emma

Emma finds that despite her good salary she doesn't really have any
savings, and in fact she has some debts on credit cards from her love of
eating out, nights on the town, shopping for clothes, and the big holiday
to Australia she had earlier in the year. She decides to cut down on luxuries for the next six months – the time it will take her to work through
this book. For her this means she won't eat out more than once a month
– she'll invite friends round for dinner from time to time instead as she
loves cooking and it's cheaper (especially as they bring the booze!). She
won't buy any new clothes in that time, and she won't travel abroad for
her next holiday in a couple of months, she'll spend a quiet week at her
parents' in Cornwall – and will even be able to use the time to work on
her business! At first she'll use the money she saves to pay off her credit
card, then she'll open a savings account and try to save as much as possible to help her once her business is up and running.

What do you know?

In Week Five we're going to look at your business idea, or help you to
think of one. To do this it helps to know what you know.

Make a list of your specialist knowledge. What do you know as a result
of your work (retailing or manufacturing, sales or accounting, the ball-
bearing industry or the fashion industry etc.)? What do you know as

a result of your hobbies (cooking, writing, sport etc.)? What do you know as a result of your education?

Emma knows about:

- Marketing, from her current job.

- The financial services industry, from her current job.

- English literature, from university.

- Food, from her favourite hobby – cooking good food and eating out in nice restaurants.

Who do you know?

It's often said that 'it's not what you know, it's who you know'. This is actually true – but not in the way these people mean. They mean that knowing a politician, a powerful business person or someone really rich or famous is what matters. It's not. What can really help you is knowing someone who has specialist knowledge in your chosen industry, someone who understands business in general or, even better, someone who has done what you want to do – start a business. And anyone you know can be helpful in some way, whether that's for providing advice, being a test customer, or putting the word out to people they know.

Make a long list now of people you know, however vaguely. Family, friends, friends of your family, friends of friends, colleagues, friends of colleagues etc. Put a note next to their name of any skills or knowledge they have.

Could any of these people be a mentor to you? A mentor is someone who has some experience in business in general, and a bit of life experience that's made them wise. They agree that you can meet them from time to time to ask questions or test your ideas out on them, and they'll give you feedback from their experience.

Having a good mentor can make a really positive difference in your business. If there is someone who has some experience, and who you really like and trust, then ask them to be your mentor. They'll be very flattered. You could also approach someone who you don't already know but who you respect – perhaps a local businessperson, or someone in the industry you're interested in.

Steve McDermott, the motivational guru, also suggests that you can have an imaginary mentor. Pick someone who is the best of the best at what you want to do (they don't even have to be living!), and find out as much as you can about them. Then, when you have a question, imagine what advice they would give you. It's amazing what insights you can get by imagining yourself in their shoes.

Emma decides to have two mentors: her real one, her boyfriend's father, Simon, who runs his own printing business, and an imaginary one, Anita Roddick. Emma has long admired Anita for having the vision and the drive to set up The Body Shop and she has read books and magazine articles about her. She'd like to run a business with similar values, so will use imaginary advice from Anita to get that part of the business right.

The list of all the people you know will also come in useful throughout all the stages of planning and starting your business, so keep it safe and refer to it regularly when you need to find some advice, access to a particular company or contact, or some other kind of help.

THIS WEEK'S TO DO LIST

- ☐ Complete the time sheet to evaluate how you spend your time now.

- ☐ Work out when you're going to spend time on your business. Book time for the next month into your diary.

- ☐ Complete the finance worksheets. Seek advice if necessary.

- ☐ Order your credit records from the agencies using the contacts on p.30.

- ☐ Make a list of your knowledge and skills.

- ☐ List the people you know and their knowledge and skills.

- ☐ Decide who you would like to be your mentor and approach them.

THIS WEEK'S RECOMMENDED READING

Money Magic, by Alvin Hall (Hodder & Stoughton).

Rich Dad, Poor Dad, by Robert Kiyosaki and Sharon Lechter (Business Plus).

LIST OF CONTACTS

Citizens Advice Bureau: **www.citizensadvice.org.uk**

Consumer Credit Counselling Service: **www.cccs.co.uk**

National Debtline: **www.nationaldebtline.co.uk**

Callcredit credit reference agency:

www.callcredit.co.uk/stat-report-online

Consumer Services, Callcredit Ltd, PO Box 491, Leeds LS3 1WZ. Enclose a cheque for £2 payable to Callcredit Ltd.

Equifax credit reference agency:

www.equifax.co.uk/Products/credit/statutory-report.html

Equifax Ltd, Credit File Advice Centre, PO Box 1140, Bradford BD1 5US. Enclose a cheque for £2 payable to Equifax Ltd.

Experian credit reference agency:

www.experian.co.uk/consumer/statutory-report.html

Customer Support Centre, Experian Ltd, PO Box 8000, Nottingham NG80 7WF. Enclose a cheque for £2 payable to Experian Ltd.

GLOSSARY

Net Worth: This is how much money you have after subtracting your liabilities (debt) from your assets (savings, investments). It can be positive if you have spare money, or negative if you are in debt overall. See value 'C' on your Personal Asset Statement on p.33.

Statutory Credit Report: Statutory means that this is something that parliament has made a law about. In this case, the Data Protection Act and the Consumer Credit Act say that the credit reference agencies have to provide you with a copy of the information they hold on you within seven working days of receiving your request accompanied by the maximum fee of £2.

Credit Reference Agencies: These are companies that gather information about your financial activities. They record information provided to them by your bank, your credit and store card providers, companies that have given you loans, etc. They also record judgments against you in court on financial matters, perhaps if a utility company has claimed an unpaid bill etc. There is no such thing as a credit blacklist. Each financial institution that assesses your credit record does so slightly differently.

DOCUMENTS

The reality of how you spend your time in a week

	Sun	Mon	Tue	Wed	Thu	Fri	Sat
00.00							
01.00							
02.00							
03.00							
04.00							
05.00							
06.00							
07.00							
08.00							
09.00							
10.00							
11.00							
12.00							
13.00							
14.00							
15.00							
16.00							
17.00							
18.00							
19.00							
20.00							
21.00							
22.00							
23.00							

Use these standard symbols:

S=Sleep; **TV**=Watching television; **E**=Eating; **Tr**=Travelling; **F**=Family time; **W**=Work (current day job); **B**=Work (on your new business)

Your own symbols:

PERSONAL ASSET STATEMENT   Figures   Totals

Property
Value of house

Savings/Insurance
Insurance policies (surrender value)
Bank/building society savings
Shares and investments

Other Assets
Car value
Other: 1: _____
Other: 2: _____
Other: 3: _____

TOTAL ASSETS
TOTAL =
FIGURE (A)

Liabilities
Total left to pay on mortgage
Total outstanding on overdraft
Total left to pay on loan(s)
Total left to pay on credit card(s)
Total other outstanding debt

TOTAL LIABILITIES
TOTAL =
FIGURE (B)

TOTAL ASSETS – TOTAL LIABILITIES   (A)–(B) = FIGURE (C)

If Figure (C) is positive, that's good.
If Figure (C) is negative by a little, then do what you can to pay off some of your debt.
If Figure (C) is negative by a lot, then get some advice from one of the sources listed in the 'List of Contacts' section.

MONTHLY BUDGET

	With your current income	Working full time in your own business
Income		
Take-home Pay		Blanked Out – calculated below
Partner's Income		
Other Income		
TOTAL INCOME Figure **(D)**		
Expenditure		
Mortgage/Rent		
Council Tax		
Electricity		
Water		
Gas/Oil		
Telephone		
Home Insurance		
Other Bills		
Groceries		
Lunches/Snacks		
Other Eating Out		
Entertainment		
Sport/Gym		
Holidays		
Presents		
Clothes		
Car Running Costs		
Other Transport		
TV Licence		
Internet Access		
Children(!)		
Debt Repayments		
Other 1		
Other 2		
Other 3		
Other 4		
TOTAL EXPENDITURE Figure **(E)**		
DIFFERENCE (D)–(E) =		

Under the column for 'With your current income', the end result (Difference) shows the following:

- If it's positive, you can start repaying more of your debt or, if you have none, saving some money towards starting your business.
- If it's negative, you need to get some advice from one of the organisations listed in the 'List of Contacts' section. You're living beyond your means and getting further into debt each month. Cut back on the luxuries.

Under the column for 'Working full time in your own business', the difference is likely to be negative, and this shows the minimum amount you have to pay yourself from your business each month in order not to get into financial difficulty.

4

Week Four:
Start Learning

This week you'll start building your entrepreneurial skills: positive attitude, networking, spotting opportunities, selling, negotiating and perseverance.

In many books about starting a business you'll find a little test at the front titled 'Have you got what it takes to be an entrepreneur?' They ask questions like 'Do you enjoy taking risks?' and get you to circle a number from 1 to 5 and add up your score at the end of the test.

Such tests are fine and entertaining in *Cosmopolitan* magazine when it's to find out which character out of *Sex and the City* you are most like – but it's plain silly to try and pigeon-hole people into some kind of stereotype about what entrepreneurs are like.

This book, however, does contain one test for the one vital characteristic of entrepreneurs, and you've already been secretly tested. If you don't have this characteristic you will fail in business; if you do have it you will greatly increase your chances of success.

Congratulations, the good news is you've passed the test! You have picked up this book, looked through it, bought it – and are reading it. This demonstrates that you have a willingness to learn and a thirst for knowledge.

A desire to learn is the one vital characteristic of entrepreneurs. It is, if you think about it, the only thing that can't be taught. Everything else you can pick up along the way.

Sharpening your entrepreneurial skills

This week you'll get going with a number of exercises to develop your natural entrepreneurial abilities. You'll start these activities this week, but you also need to keep them up in future weeks – it's like playing a musical instrument or a sport, you have to continually practise.

Positive attitude

Successful people in any field are those who are positive. They believe their ideas will work, they believe that people are generally good, and they expect things to be fun. Years of corporate grind, or even just the fact that you live in the UK, may have taught you to be cynical and pessimistic. You need to relearn such childish pleasures as being happy, and believing that things will work out.

From now on, get in training to be more positive. When people ask how you are, say 'great' or 'fantastic' instead of 'fine' or 'not bad'. Actively look for things to be happy about. Decide to be happy.

It may not come easy at first, but that's what practice and training are all about.

Networking

The first skill to learn is how to build and maintain your network of contacts. Last week you looked at your existing network. Now, how can you increase the reach of your network? Step one is to go to things. Do you ever turn down invitations to things because you can't be bothered talking to all those people, you feel shy, or you're too tired? Start accepting a few more invitations, and practise going round talking to as many people as possible.

A few tips for networking at events:

- Be there to listen not talk; steer the conversation around to be about the person you meet rather than you. That's the only way to learn stuff.

- Keep your radar tuned for opportunities (see 'Spotting opportunities' on the next page). How can you help them solve a problem? Your solution may not directly benefit you – it may be to put them in touch with a friend of yours, or to recommend a supplier – but you will benefit by practising spotting opportunities and networking. If you're known for genuinely helping other people with no self-interest, people will feel they would like to help you too.

- Don't try to sell, just get to know people.

- Get rid of bores. Every event has them. They're normally negative people who just drone on and on about themselves. Be polite, but move on to someone else.

- Don't be a bore! Every now and then during the conversation, listen to yourself. Is it all 'me me me', 'my complaint' and 'my opinion'? If so, change to asking questions about the other person.

You'll soon learn how to make events useful and fun for you.

There are some networking clubs that are only about networking for sales, and they go about it single-mindedly. You'll have to decide whether this is your cup of tea. It's not really mine. I prefer to go along to general business events, and then use the opportunity to meet people for the sake of getting to know them.

Another way of building your network is maintaining your existing network. Make sure you stay in touch with people, and that they know what you're doing and what you want. Then they can put you in touch with people in their network. Keep a contacts file and constantly add new people you meet, with a few notes about them and how you can help them and they can help you.

Spotting opportunities

There are opportunities everywhere you look – you just need to let your imagination roam free, like you did when you were a child.

Look for opportunities all day, however crazy. On your journey to work, how would you develop your business if you ran the train or bus company, or you made cars or maintained roads? At lunchtime in winter, what opportunities are there for healthy, hot, snack lunches? Everywhere you go, someone has a business that serves you – how could they do it better?

You may already have the idea for your business, but this exercise is still useful in helping you refine that idea, and spot the opportunities to maximise the success of your idea. If you know you want to start a business, but don't yet have an idea, this exercise is going to be really useful for you, and next week you'll develop these skills to generate some ideas for your business.

As I write this I'm on an early morning train from York to London. The train is busy, and a lot of people use this service to commute to London on a regular basis. The train company would obviously like to increase their revenues per passenger (I know this because they keep putting the prices up, persuading more and more people to travel by car!). So how could they increase revenues innovatively and persuade people to travel by train?

OK, let's have a five-minute brainstorm. The key is not to criticise the ideas, or throw any out at this stage. Write them down however silly they are.

So, if I ran this train company I would:

1. Put an extra carriage on trains that is a gym. The carriage could have cycling machines, rowing machines and resistance apparatus. It could have a couple of shower cubicles and changing rooms (these carriages are quite big). People could pay a supplement on their ticket to be able to access the gym carriage, and spend their two-hour journey exercising rather than wasting time. The added benefit for them is they could leave the house early in the morning without showering, get on the train in their gym gear, exercise and then shower and change for their day.

2. Similar to the above idea, have an on-board hairdressers/barbers.

3. Introduce a business ticketing system for people who don't need a season ticket because they don't travel every day, but who travel often enough that it's a real pain to queue at the counter or phone up and wait on hold every time they need a ticket. You'd be issued with a swipe card, like a credit card, and there would be card readers at every station. You swipe the card at the station where you get on, and again at the station you get off at. The guard has a mini card reader to check you have a valid card on the train. Each month you receive a statement for the journeys you have made and they take payment by direct debit. (Since the first edition of this book, the Oyster system was introduced in London – so now they just have to expand it to all trains!)

4. There are some noisy children on board. One at the end of the carriage is screaming his head off at his poor embarrassed mother – and you should see the look on the face of the woman sitting opposite them. Could there be a carriage for people travelling with children? It could have facilities for nappy changing, warming bottles, a few cots, a play area, and games based on what children can spot out of the window on the route.

When you've finished, you can then go through the ideas and review them, looking for problems and filtering them down. Now number 2 is plainly daft because, although a lot of business people find it a chore to make the time to get their hair done, not many people will want sharp objects around their head on a high-speed train that's shaking all over the place. Number 4 probably doesn't have much revenue potential on a commuter train – although it would be very welcome on the trains down to Cornwall in the school holidays. Numbers 1 and 3 could be interesting to explore further.

These two stages of brainstorming are called 'Green Light' and 'Red Light'. During the Green Light stage you write down absolutely anything that pops into your mind. You don't reject any idea, no matter how ridiculous. In the Red Light stage you go through all your ideas and look for problems. You then refine or reject the idea.

Practise this constantly. Wherever you go, try to generate ideas for how things could be improved – on the way to work, at the sandwich shop for lunch, at the pub in the evening, when you go out for the day at the weekend, and so on.

The other key way of spotting opportunities is to listen to other people. Listen out for problems they have, or unfulfilled wishes. What ideas can you think of to solve their problems or provide them with what they wish for?

You'll hear people say things like: 'I wish I could find good low-alcohol beer in this country like you can in Scandinavia.' (This is something

I've said since the first edition of this book. Hopefully someone reading this will finally take the hint!)

What are the opportunities? Well, at a basic level you could import nicer low-alcohol beer. At the next level you would license the brand and recipe for one of the Scandinavian brands and start producing it over here. At an advanced level you could develop your own recipe, build your own low-alcohol brewery and build a bigger business and brand.

Try to think of three opportunities by the end of the week. Then you should make sure that you write down one idea for a business opportunity every week. It doesn't have to be perfect, but it's the fact that you've spotted it that matters.

These aren't necessarily ideas you will actually turn into a business – you're just exercising your brain, and developing your opportunity-spotting muscle.

Selling

You're never going to get very far with your business unless you learn a bit about selling. You don't have to become like the dreaded used-car salesperson – in fact it's best if you don't – but you do have to get comfortable with selling and sharpen your skills. It's all about practice.

So what can you do to practise? Here are some ideas to choose from:

- Take a pitch at a local car-boot sale, and sell old books, records, clothes, ornaments – anything!

- See if you can get more of a selling role for a while in your current job. Your boss won't often get requests to spend a bit of time on the phone or out selling to customers, and they'll probably leap at the idea.

- Can you help out in a local shop or other business on Saturdays for a few weeks doing some sales?

Also it's well worth getting some books or audio programmes on selling.

Negotiating

Everything is negotiable! That's the entrepreneur's mantra. You're going to need to negotiate to get the best from your suppliers, and negotiate to get the best from your customers.

It's not all about negotiating on price though – it's about value. That is the best balance between all that you need and want the product or service to do, and the price. You don't want to be like a friend of mine who returned from the supermarket delighted that she'd saved money by buying ten tins of tuna for the price of five in a special offer – indisputably a bargain, but unfortunately she doesn't like tuna.

There are plenty of opportunities to practise negotiating – but it may take some guts or cheek from you at first.

Negotiate more at work, whether it's with colleagues, suppliers or customers. Ask for a little bit more of everything, or for a cheaper price. Get a bit bolder and ask for bigger things.

Go to your local market and try negotiating there to get a discount or something extra thrown in.

Another great way to practise negotiating is to wait for one of those telesales phone calls that normally annoy you. When you next get one talk to them for a while, let them pitch their offer to you and then start negotiating. Because they've intruded on you at home, you can feel free to push your negotiating to the extreme for extra training. Beat them down as low as you can, get freebies thrown in, whatever you like. The best bit is you can be as bold as you like because you don't want whatever it is anyway. When you've practised for a while ask for something really outrageous, and when they can't agree to that you can finish the call. Even asking for something so outrageous is great practice with your negotiating confidence, because it'll feel awful to do at first.

The first golden rule of negotiating is that if you don't ask, you don't get.

The second golden rule of negotiating in normal circumstances is that no one should get conned. If either of you walk away from the deal and feel you've been had, then you both lose out. You won't do business with that person again. Make sure every deal you do is one where everybody is happy.

From now on practise negotiating at every opportunity. Always try to get something thrown into the deal as a bonus or something off the price of anything you buy.

Perseverance

Finally you have to learn not to give up. This is the difference between successful entrepreneurs and those who try and fail. You will have numerous problems in the course of starting your business, and it may even seem like there is no solution, but there always is, and it comes with persistence.

I have friends who have very successful businesses now, but who went through very tough times and nearly lost everything. Despite the huge obstacles in their way, they were convinced that they could pull through, so they persevered and they succeeded. Lesser people would have given up very quickly.

Remember though that perseverance and persistence aren't about shouting or throwing a tantrum until you get your way. It's about calmly and quietly navigating a way through against all obstacles.

Use your brain, use your negotiating skills, use all your diplomacy and more than your normal supply of patience. Just don't give up.

Find out about local banks, accountants and lawyers

While you're out networking, this is a useful task you can carry out. In building your business you will need a bank account, an accountant or book-keeper, and probably a lawyer too. You're bound to meet some when you're out at networking events – to be honest you won't be able to swing even a small kitten without hitting three or four.

However, the best way to find a good banker and advisers is through personal recommendation, so talk to real business people at these events, and people you know. Who do they use? Why? What do they think of them?

In the UK there are a limited number of banks, and I've heard good and bad stories about all of them. In reality a lot depends on the individual bank managers, so it's all about the person – and that's why it's good to get a recommendation from another business owner who has dealt with them.

When it comes to finding an accountant or lawyer, don't go for the big firms at this stage. You can go to them when you're bigger, but they are too expensive for you now! Find out about smaller local firms.

For now just gather names and contact details from different people you meet over the next month or two – you'll be contacting them later to arrange a first meeting.

Emma

Emma decides that she could practise her sales skills, and earn some money to pay off her credit cards, by sorting through all her things and taking anything she doesn't need any more to the local car-boot sale at the weekend. She sorts out a big pile of things including clothes, shoes, a couple of handbags, books and her old bike.

That Wednesday morning before work, she goes to a breakfast networking event run by her local chamber of commerce and gets chatting to a couple of other local businesswomen. They ask her about her work and she describes her plans to start a business, including her idea to practise her sales skills this weekend. The others are impressed by her determination, and say they should have a similar clear out of all of their stuff, but they'd never have the time to run a car-boot stall. Emma offers that if they have a sort-out by Friday she'll pick up their things and sell them on her stall, and they could split the earnings. 'It's a deal!' the others say, and the arrangements are made.

At lunchtime later that day Emma decides to do some brainstorming on how she would improve on the networking event if she were to run one. This is to practise her opportunity spotting. She comes up with:

1. When each person arrives, she or one of her team would take them over and introduce them to a group, so everyone gets involved in a conversation straight away.

2. When registering for the event, she'd ask people a few questions – about their hobbies, what book they're reading at the moment etc, and have bigger name stickers on which she'd print some of these things – as conversation starters.

3. She'd play business card bingo. Everyone puts five business cards in a jar, and then draws out five cards at random. The first person to have met and talked to all five people whose cards they have is the winner.

4. She'd noticed at this morning's event that the people who got to meet and speak to most of the guests were the catering staff who went round topping up the tea and coffee. It was a great way to make an introduction into a group of people. So she'd have guests serving themselves, and encouraged to go around the room offering top-ups to others. It'd save money too!

5. She wants to encourage people to come regularly, so anyone who has been to five or more events in a row would get a special colour badge and be regarded as a kind of respected member that others could get advice from.

Saturday comes and she has a successful day at the boot fair, taking over £150, of which she has to give £47 to the other women whose things she sold. She got to practise her negotiation skills when it came to selling the bike, and got £50 for it after negotiating a man up from £25.

She went home tired but satisfied, and feeling like she'd made a dent in her debt as well as having learned a lot.

Shared Experiences

Robert Hart wanted to start his own business to develop a better design of scuba-diving equipment. Once he had this vision in mind, inspiration came from the most unlikely of places:

'As I was walking up a platform at Liverpool Street Station in London one day, I saw hundreds of different rucksacks that were being worn by men, women and children, all in different colours, shapes and sizes, and I thought, well, here's a format that has been accepted for over ten years

▶

and has in many ways replaced things like handbags, and how would it be if we could make one of these work under water. And so that's why I chose the format of a rucksack to be the new type of scuba kit. Simple, easy to use and attractive.'

As a result, Robert set up Mini Breather Holdings plc.

Peter Wilkinson is one of the entrepreneurs who started Freeserve, and has also got a string of other major successes under his belt. He features quite highly in the *Sunday Times* Rich List. What does he think are his key skills?

'Grim, grim determination to succeed; I try to do it in as pleasant a way as possible. I don't lose my rag, I don't shout and scream at people; I try to motivate people to want to do it, rather than force them. I think my only skill is spotting an opportunity and actually making it happen. But it takes huge amounts of energy and determination, but you've got to do it 'cos if you don't your business is just finished.'

Richard Wiseman is the author of *The Luck Factor*, a book that looks at how successful people make their own 'luck':

'I think that people who achieve more have got a strong social network, so they go out there, they meet people and therefore when they do hit a problem when they are trying to develop something they can tap into a greater social circle than most people. So, that's number one – get out there and talk to people.

'The second thing is people who have got a positive attitude. So you have people who see the best in situations, they see opportunities where other people don't. They feel positive. They are not the gloomy depressed ones. So positive intent will get you there. I also think that a strong level of emotional intelligence, to use a jargon word, somebody who is in tune and recognises what is happening – someone who has a strong level of self-awareness.

'So after that I think that people have to persevere, they have got to stick at it. People give up too soon. The ones who achieve their goals are the ones when they hit obstacles don't just give up and pack it in, they try again. They find another route. They are versatile, they are flexible, they

have got new ways of finding solutions. Then it's about being in control of your own destiny. Accepting responsibility for who you are and being the person who drives the bus, not the person who is being driven.'

THIS WEEK'S TO DO LIST

- ☐ Be positive!

- ☐ Get networking, either by accepting invitations that you already get, or by contacting the networking organisations (see the next page for contact details) and arranging to go to one or two meetings or events. Most will let you go along to one or two without becoming a full member, so that you can see if you would like to join. You'll probably have to pay between £10 and £20 to go along. Don't shell out for membership yet!

- ☐ Consciously look for opportunities. Write down at least three by the end of the week.

- ☐ Organise a way to practise selling – at work, at a car-boot sale, anywhere.

- ☐ Negotiate some great deals for yourself.

- ☐ Persevere!

- ☐ Find out about local bankers, accountants and lawyers.

- ☐ Remember to keep updating your blog each week at **www.weekbyweek.net/startyourbusiness**

THIS WEEK'S RECOMMENDED READING

The Luck Factor, by Richard Wiseman (Arrow).

The author has conducted extensive research into what successful people do differently that makes them more 'lucky' than others. This book includes his findings, and guidance on how you can learn to become more lucky.

LIST OF CONTACTS

For networking events:

Your local Chamber of Commerce. Google for details.

Junior Chamber UK: **www.jciuk.org.uk**

This is a fantastic organisation of really positive, ambitious young people (it limits membership to the under-40s). They are either on the career fast track in big companies, or running their own businesses. The organisation is about personal development, networking and having fun – and having been to one of their conferences I can guarantee that the last part of that is taken just as importantly as the rest! They have local meetings, and you'd be more than welcome to go along and see how you like it.

Professional bodies for your industry or profession:

If you don't already know these organisations, search on the internet.

5 Week Five:
The Founders

This week you'll decide on the founding team for your business.

A lot of people seem to have a picture of entrepreneurs as Lone Rangers, but in many successful businesses in reality there is a small team of co-founders who each bring different skills to the new enterprise.

Starting a business is very hard work, and can feel quite lonely at times. Even just having one other person in your business from the start can make a big difference – to your sanity as well as your success. It'll be a great help to be able to share the workload between you. You can also support each other through the tough times, and celebrate together in the good times.

The founders of Innocent Drinks say that having a founding team of three, each with a different skill-set, was a vital part of their success. I hear the same from many entrepreneurs – as well as hearing from solo founders just how tough it was to do it alone.

There's an African proverb that says: 'If you want to go quickly, go alone. If you want to go far, go together.'

Deciding what's right for you

It may be that you really do want to do this on your own at this stage, and if you're sure about that, it's fine. Do talk it over with your mentor though.

Solo founders can skip ahead to the section 'Write about the founders' on p.53, and you'll have some spare time this week – I suggest reading at least one biography of an entrepreneur you admire and making notes of things you can learn from them.

Choosing co-founders

Choosing co-founders really is like dating and getting married. You have a far greater chance of lasting success if you don't rush into things and take the time to see how you cope together with the challenges that can present themselves. I once had a very bad experience with co-founders who were great to know as friends and in the early stages of running a small business – but when the company started becoming large and successful they didn't know what to do, and began behaving irrationally and doing things that made them feel more in control.

It caused some big problems and a messy split before I was eventually able to end up in one company that was large and fast growing, and they were able to end up in a much smaller business that they felt more comfortable with.

This is a fairly common story in fast-growth businesses, and highlights the importance of bringing in co-founders very slowly and carefully – making sure there's clear agreement that one person is in charge, and what to do in the event of disagreement.

Is there anyone that you would like to work with? A friend, a family member, someone you work with now? Have a think about what they would be like to work with, how you rate their work, how hardworking they are, and what skills they could bring to the business. Can you imagine working twelve-hour days with them, and then still wanting to go to the pub to chat over the day?

If you decide it would be a good idea, approach them about it. They'll hopefully be flattered, as it shows a great deal of respect for them and their work. Take them for a drink or a meal and tell them all about your ambitions. At first they'll be a bit stunned, but gradually they'll start coming up with questions, concerns, and then even ideas.

Don't rush into anything. You both need lots of time to think about it, but as you don't have to give up your day jobs yet you can work on the business together with little risk to see how you get on.

Decide on roles

Aside from who is to lead the team, if there are going to be two or more of you then you need to specify what your roles are.

These are some of the things to do in your business. Add your own thoughts to this list, and then split the tasks up between you:

- Selling to your customers – actually clinching the deals.

- Managing the money and the admin.

- Buying from your suppliers.

- Actually doing what it is that your business does (you might all end up involved in this at first), or managing the people who do this work.

- Promoting your business to potential customers using PR, advertising, promotional stunts, special offers, leaflets, websites etc.

Agreeing terms

To ensure that your founding team works together smoothly, it's important that you establish some ground rules at the very start:

Equality. The amount of the business you own and what you will get paid need to reflect what you put into the company. If at all possible put in equal amounts of work, equal amounts of initial investment, own an equal share of the business, take equal pay, and so on. This helps to remove so many problems further down the line.

If this really isn't possible, then carefully document what you've agreed each person will get and in return for what – how much each person is investing, how much time they will spend working on the business, and what percentage of the business they will own.

Leadership. There can only be one leader in the business. This should be the person who is better at being positive, seeing the bigger picture, the long-term vision, and communicating it to others. The other people will all be part of the management team, taking roles suitable to their talents and experience, but there needs to be a leader who is allowed to make the key decisions after having heard the views of the others. One person being the leader does not affect equality – they shouldn't start to think they're above everyone else or that their contribution is more special or their opinions matter more. Their role is to support the founding team, remind them of the ambition you all share, and help to develop a consensus about the way to get there. It's just a different role in a team of equals.

It may seem a bit too formal, but it's well worth having a simple written agreement at this stage to set out:

- Who is to be involved.

- What their involvement will be.

- The fact that the work everyone does will become the property of the company once formed.

- What shares/ownership of the company each person will have when it is formed.

- What will happen if people leave before the company is formed.

This will be enough for now. You can then draft a more detailed shareholders' agreement at a later stage when you know more about the business.

Decide on pay

You'll have done your monthly budget back in Week Three, and now is the time to use that, along with the details of any savings you have, to work out how much you will pay yourself, if anything, from the company.

This will be a careful balance between not taking too much cash out of the business and making sure that you're not going to run into problems or be distracted by personal finance issues when you really should be working!

This pay will only come into effect once you start work in the business full time at a later date.

Get everyone in the founding team to do the same exercise, and it's also something to discuss with your mentor.

Emma

Emma decides that she'd like to find a business partner to start her business with, as she thinks she'll be too lonely moving from a big company to just being on her own. She's also terrible at managing money and any administrative tasks.

Her friend Alan works in the accounts team at the same company, and they worked together brilliantly on a project last year, which is when they got to know each other. He's one of the people who have been encouraging Emma to start her own business. He's very good at the skills where Emma is weak.

Emma decides to approach him and he's very flattered, but a bit nervous about the risks. They agree to work together on the planning and to defer the final decision until later. It's agreed that he will have a 40 per cent stake in the company if he joins, investing 40 per cent of the money, and that he will take care of the accounts, admin and negotiating with suppliers.

Remember

Your start-up team are not there for you to boss around. You need to let them contribute ideas, shape their part of the business, and grow their skills in order for them to be as excited and committed to the company as you.

Write about the founders

Write a one- or two-page report on your founding team. Give a brief description of each of you, including career background, experience in this marketplace, specialist skills etc. Why are you the right people to run this business?

You should also each write a CV to attach to this document.

It's important to write this up, as you'll be using this document later.

THIS WEEK'S TO DO LIST

- ☐ Decide if you want to start up alone or with others.
- ☐ Talk to people about joining you in business.
- ☐ Form your start-up team.
- ☐ Decide on roles.
- ☐ Write up a founders' agreement.
- ☐ Write up a founders' document.
- ☐ Each of you should write a CV.

THIS WEEK'S RECOMMENDED READING

Brilliant CV: What Employers Want to See and How You Should Write It, by Dr Jim Bright and Joanne Earl (Pearson).

6 Week Six:
The Idea

This week you'll begin the first steps of developing the idea for your business, as well as following up on some of the work from previous weeks.

Every single business you have ever heard of started as the idea of an entrepreneurial individual or small team – even the major global brands.

For example, I originally wrote this chapter in 2004 while sitting in a Starbucks café in London after a day of meetings. Starbucks is an internationally recognised brand and there are thousands of their coffee bars across the world. They are such a huge company – not a small business like yours or mine. It must have been started by a big corporation.

As it happens the chain of coffee shops was the idea of Howard Schultz, who fell in love with Italian coffee bar culture on a visit to the country and decided to try bringing it to Seattle, then, when it worked, to the rest of the United States, then to the rest of the world. If you're old enough to remember what cafés in the UK were like before Starbucks – with instant coffee in styrofoam cups and no reason to linger – then you'll know what a revolution this company brought to the world.

It was a hot day so instead of coffee I bought a fruit drink made by Innocent Drinks. The company was started by a group of three twenty-something friends who weren't satisfied in their corporate careers and wanted to start a venture together. They liked fruit smoothies, and made them at home, but were frustrated that the only commercial drinks they could buy were full of additives and lacked the flavour of their own drinks. They went into business to make wholesome, tasty fruit drinks, and are now very successful as a result.

So we have two different-sized businesses – a global brand and a small but fast-growing British company. They have been selected as examples simply because I happened to be using their products as I wrote this chapter, but both were started by entrepreneurial people with an idea.

If we look at the café business in the UK now, as I write this second edition in 2012, we find that big Starbucks-style chains have become the norm – but, in reaction to that, entrepreneurs have found a market for small artisan coffee shops, offering handmade cakes and good coffee in less corporate surroundings. There are hundreds, if not thousands, of these individualistic entrepreneurial cafés across the country now. So ideas go in cycles of evolution.

Think about objects around you now, or products or services you are using. What do you know about the business behind them? Who started it and why?

The point is that every business starts with someone like you, with an idea. There are some books suggested on p.65 that tell the stories of these people. They make great reading and you'll be inspired by what someone just like you can achieve.

If you already have an idea for your business, then it's still worth reading this week and doing the exercises, because you can refine your idea to be even better.

You don't need to be a beardy-weirdy inventor

Before we start brainstorming for ideas, I need to dispel a bit of a myth that's always existed about entrepreneurship and has been exacerbated by TV shows like *Dragons' Den*. You don't need to be a crazy inventor creating some brand new weird contraption in order to start a successful business.

Did you notice something about the two successful businesses I highlighted above? The founders didn't invent the product or service at the centre of their business. Howard Schultz didn't invent the coffee bar – he liked them in Italy and brought them to the USA, adapted for American tastes. The Innocent founders didn't invent the idea of making drinks from fruit – they just improved them for a target audience who wanted something without additives.

Let's look at other businesses. Did McDonald's invent the burger? Did British Airways invent the aeroplane? Did Subway invent the sandwich? Did Harry Ramsden's invent fish and chips? Did Nike invent the training shoe? No.

You don't need to hide in your garden shed for the next six months inventing some crazy machine – there are thousands of opportunities to build a successful business by serving customers in a better way with existing ideas.

There are always solid businesses to be built as shops, cafés, restaurants, photographers, design agencies, web agencies, PR firms, estate agents and so on. But there are still plenty of ways to innovate within a traditional industry.

Adapting an existing idea: improving location, luxury or love

There are three ways to build a successful business by adapting and improving an existing product or service for your target audience. You've probably guessed from the heading what they are. So what do they mean?

Improving location

You can adapt an idea locally by bringing it from any place to any other place. In most cases this will be to or from where you are, an area you know.

We've already seen an example of this with Starbucks, but there are plenty more. Another example is YO! Sushi, whose founder Simon

Woodroffe brought the concept of a Japanese 'kaiten' sushi bar that delivered food to customers via a conveyor belt to the masses. It has become the most famous sushi brand in the UK.

What products or services exist in other countries or other places in your own country, but not where you are? Could you bring them to your area?

What products or services exist in your country or city, but not elsewhere? Could you take them there?

Another way of improving location is by taking the point of sale of a common product to a more convenient place for the customer. Could you go and sell to customers in their homes, like Avon, Ann Summers and the mail-order catalogue companies? Could you make it easier for customers to buy products by phone, like Direct Line insurance? Could you make it easier for customers to order online like Amazon? Could you sell to people at work, like the countless sandwich vans that tour business parks across the country?

Improving luxury

You can adapt an idea by increasing the level of luxury to make it more exclusive, or by reducing the level of luxury to bring the product or service to a wider audience.

easyJet and Ryanair saw the opportunity to bring air travel to a much wider audience by stripping out all the luxuries to reduce the price. IKEA saw the same opportunity with furniture.

Meanwhile a number of small, independent hotels and restaurants around the UK are seeing the opportunity to attract high-value customers by increasing the level of luxury and becoming desirable weekend retreats for busy working couples, or fashionable places to stay in cities during the week.

What product or service can you add luxury to in order to serve your target audience?

What product or service can you remove luxury from in order to attract your target audience?

Improving love

An increasing opportunity is to adapt an idea by adding love. There is a real trend for consumers wanting to deal with companies that have a personality, an obvious love for what they do, and an obvious love for their customers.

I believe this is a really important opportunity, and one that is particularly suited to entrepreneurs.

Take a look at the website of **www.innocentdrinks.co.uk** – or even better, go and try their drinks and read their bottles. Feel the love!

So what have they done in order to create a business with added love? They had a passion for that subject anyway. They built the business out of their own needs. They've then made sure that their passion isn't hidden away behind expensive corporate-style marketing brochures and websites. They write the copy for the website and their marketing materials in-house, they design their own adverts, they try to be in contact with their customers rather than hiding behind call centres, and they have fun!

But the most important thing they ever do is when they recruit people. They only hire people who share their passion for the subject and their positive attitude to the business and the customer. One person cannot build a business on love if the rest of the team are jobsworths.

What are your passions in life?

Could you adapt a business idea in this area and add some love?

You can also adapt an idea by removing love, but really, who would want to?

Using your skills

You can develop a business idea based on your skills. These needn't just be related to the job you do now. What are your general skills in life? In your hobbies? At home? And at work?

Spotting opportunities

You've been practising spotting opportunities since last week. Have any of those inspired you? What problems are people facing? What unfulfilled needs do they have? How can you solve that?

The brainstorm

So, now it's time to think of some business ideas. Remember that this is still worth doing if you already have your business idea, as you need to exercise your entrepreneurial skills – and you could even come up with some improvements to your initial thoughts.

You had a go at brainstorming last week (and perhaps it's something you've done before anyway), but this week we're going to do it for real to help you discover your business idea.

To refresh your memory, brainstorming is done in two stages. The first part is the 'Green Light' stage in which you just let your mind wander all over the place, coming up with really bizarre ideas. You don't criticise or select them in any way. You write them all down no matter how stupid they might be. If you're brainstorming with anyone else, you must make sure that you don't criticise each other's ideas at this stage. Anyone should feel able to contribute anything.

The second part is the 'Red Light' stage in which you look at all your ideas more critically. You quickly weed out the daft ones, then you might adapt or reject some others. You're then left with a core of potentially good ideas. Some of them might even shine out as brilliant ideas. Look more carefully at each one of these. What could be the problems with each one? How difficult would each be to start as a business? What are the advantages of each one? How much of a demand do you think there will be?

The end of the week

If you do a Green Light brainstorm every night this week and a Red Light analysis at the end of the week, you'll be amazed by the range and quality of ideas you can generate. If you think hard enough you might even get a 'Eureka!' moment.

However, it is possible that you will discard all of your ideas, or that none of them really appeal to you very much.

If this is the case then feel free to postpone going on to next week and have another week, or even more, of research, thinking and brainstorming until you hit on the perfect idea for you. You may also want to visit the website that supports this book at **www.weekbyweek.net/startyourbusiness** to view some business case studies and chat with other entrepreneurs online to get some inspiration.

Emma

Emma already has her idea. One of her big frustrations is not being able to get lunches at work that she enjoys. She likes good food, and she likes to eat healthily, but the only option that is available to her is a sandwich. The local sandwich shops don't have very inspiring ingredients, except one that is a bit more daring, but she soon gets bored of eating sandwiches every day anyway. And in winter, the only options for hot fast food aren't very healthy. She doesn't have much time at lunchtime, so she can't go and sit down at a restaurant or café – she generally eats at her desk – but she would be prepared to pay extra for being able to get something tasty and healthy made with good-quality ingredients.

While on her holiday in Australia, she found a chain of healthy fast-food shops called Sumo Salad (**www.sumosalad.com**), and fell in love with the idea.

She'd like to set up a healthy, tasty, fast-food shop, and her long-term dream is to build it into a chain of shops.

Following up from previous weeks

Your credit reports

The reports on your credit file (which you requested in Week Three) should have arrived by now from the credit reference agencies. If they haven't, then contact them to complain, as they have to provide you with your report within seven working days of receiving your request and payment.

If the reports have arrived, use the accompanying leaflet to go through each report and check what each entry means. If everything seems OK, then breathe a sigh of relief and move on.

If there are adverse entries on your credit file, then follow these steps.

If you accept that all the adverse entries are accurate, then consult your local Citizens Advice Bureau or another suitable agency (see the 'List of Contacts' in Week Three) for advice on what you should do to settle any problem that is creating an adverse entry. You can also talk directly to the organisation that has put the entry on your file to see how you can settle the matter with them so that they remove, or mark as satisfied, the adverse entry.

If you believe that an adverse entry on your credit record is incorrect, you should follow the advice given in the leaflet that accompanies the report. You can also seek help from one of the advice agencies listed in the contacts section of Week Three.

Even one slightly bad entry on your credit file can cause you huge problems these days – preventing you from opening a business bank account, trade accounts with suppliers and so on. I believe that credit reference agencies, and the companies that submit entries to them, need much tighter regulation, and that there should be more hurdles for them to jump through before they can place an adverse entry on your file. The power of credit reference agencies is a growing problem that will seriously hinder the growth of an enterprise culture in the UK.

Shared Experiences

John Barnes is a serial entrepreneur who left his job with KFC to buy one fish and chip shop in Yorkshire and turned it into a national brand – Harry Ramsden's:

'My colleague Richard and I had this idea that here were these American-style branded chicken stores being very successful in the UK and yet there was no national brand in fish and chips. I had come to

Leeds when I played football at university and seen Harry Ramsden's and it had always left this imprint on my mind as something larger than life, because it wasn't a fish and chip shop; it was this huge restaurant with chandeliers, carpets and wonderful nostalgic values. Richard had the idea that we should buy it, and turn it into a bigger brand.'

Sahar Hashemi had been working in New York, and loved the Italian-style coffee bars that were in the city. When she moved back to London she couldn't find them anywhere:

'I fell in love with the concept. I didn't see an opportunity, I just fell in love with it as a customer. I told my brother how much I missed it, and wished there was something similar in London, and it was him that spotted the opportunity, and persuaded me.'

Sahar and her brother went on to start Coffee Republic.

Tony Dorigo is a former international footballer. When his professional football career came to an end, he began looking for a business that he could run:

'I decided to try to develop an all-encompassing service, where footballers could go for all the parts missing from their lives. Initially I saw us providing all the sexy services – let's be honest, footballers like their watches, they like their plasma screens, they like their holidays – but when I looked into it further and recollected my own experiences of moving club and country, I realised that there was a lot more to it. So take the scenario of a player and his wife coming to a new country. First of all there's the flights, then the hotels, then it's finding the right areas to live in, and researching the schools. If you want the family to come over, it's sorting out hire cars. You may want a cleaner found, and a gardener. You find a lovely house, but want an extension – we have a buildings manager who will find the best quote and manage every aspect of the build. It really is anything and everything.'

He developed this into The One Club, a valuable service for VIPs.

Bill Gates started Microsoft:

'[When we started] . . . there really was no software industry, software was done sort of as an afterthought by hardware companies, the thing *that was at the centre of people's minds was the hardware. And the insight we had was that this would get flipped around where, although hardware would still be important, the thing that would drive the value of information technology would be software. So we said, okay, let's build the world's best software company.'*

Trenton Moss, founder of Webcredible:

'I was in Beijing after having been travelling for a few years, and was trying to book my return journey home on the Trans-Siberian railway, and I had the most frustrating experience on the travel company's website. It was so poorly designed it was almost unusable. Obviously a seed had been planted by this, because I woke up with a start at 5 a.m. the next morning and decided to set up a consultancy to help people design websites that are easier for their customers to use, and therefore earn them more money.'

Simon Woodroffe, founder of YO! Sushi:

'One night a Japanese friend mentioned four words I had never heard in a row before: "Conveyor Belt Sushi Bar". I was fascinated and went home that night, sat in front of the phone and thought "shall I run up a bill to phone Japan and research this?", and of course I did. Within three months I knew a great deal about them and I had this feeling inside, that although I knew logically that it was high risk, I felt certain it was going to be a big hit.'

THIS WEEK'S TO DO LIST

☐ Do a 'Green Light' brainstorm for an hour every night this week.

☐ Pack a notepad and pen in your briefcase, handbag or something else you will often be carrying with you during the week. You might have a flash of inspiration at work, on the train or anywhere else and you'll want to note it down.

- [ ] Put a notepad and pen by your bed for the same reason.
- [ ] At the end of the week, do a 'Red Light' analysis of your ideas.
- [ ] Deal with your credit reports.

THIS WEEK'S RECOMMENDED READING

Anyone Can Do It, by Bobby and Sahar Hashemi (Capstone Publishing).

One of the most straightforward and candid books about starting up.

Marketing Judo, by John Barnes and Richard Richardson (Prentice Hall Business).

Not only is this the story of how they built Harry Ramsden's into a major brand with practically no marketing budget, but they carefully analyse the key things they did and show how you can do the same in your business.

Pour Your Heart into It, by Howard Schultz and Dori Jones Yang (Hyperian).

The story behind Starbucks.

Smart Luck, by Andrew Davidson (Prentice Hall Business).

Interviews with a selection of big-name entrepreneurs, and thoughts on their common traits.

LIST OF CONTACTS

You'll need the credit reference and support agencies listed in the contacts section of Week Three.

7 Week Seven:
Idea to Opportunity

This week you'll work to assess your ideas and refine them into a real business opportunity.

Last week (or over the last few weeks if you extended last week's exercise until you got what you believe is a great idea) you worked on generating ideas for a business. You might now have one shining idea that you think is a clear winner, or a few ideas that you're trying to decide between. Either way it's fine. I'll refer to a single idea throughout this chapter, but do put all your ideas through the same exercise.

This week we're going to examine whether your idea can become an opportunity. It's a subtle, but crucial, difference. A good idea is met with people going 'Ah! That's a good idea!', whereas it's only a good opportunity if that phrase is followed by them becoming a paying customer for it.

The world has seen many would-be entrepreneurs fall by the wayside with really good ideas that weren't also good opportunities – often only after they've invested their time, savings and hard work. It's really much better to find out as early as possible whether your idea really does present you with an opportunity.

As you work through this process you may find problems with some or all of your ideas, but persevere. Review the ideas to see if you can refine them and make them more viable – or go back to the ideas generation process and create some more ideas and put them through this process too.

What is an opportunity?

To an entrepreneur an opportunity is an idea that meets a customer's need so well, in fact better than any competing ideas, that they are prepared to pay money for it.

So, first of all – you need a customer. Give some thought to whom the target customers for your idea might be. Try to be as focused as possible. If you're really saying 'everyone' then your sales and marketing will, ironically, be much harder. But if you decide, for example, that your target customers are people who love classic cars, then you can take a stall at classic car fairs, advertise in classic car magazines, join classic car forums online, and so on. So a clear focus will really help you.

Write a paragraph or two about the target customers for your idea. Are they consumers or businesspeople? How can they be identified – by geography, sector, age, lifestage or other factors? What are their needs? What are their problems?

Then, give some thought to whether your idea meets their needs. They'll want it to achieve some of the following:

- Solve a problem they have.

- Save or make them money.

- Save them time.

- Create an opportunity for them.

- Prevent something they worry about.

- Make them feel good about themselves.

- Make them look good to others.

- Provide them with enjoyment.

Honestly assess whether your idea achieves one or more of these for your target customers. Are there ways to improve the idea to meet more of these needs?

Write down the needs and desires of your customer when it comes to your idea.

Now it's time to look at the competition. What other companies are serving their needs in this way at the moment? It's incredibly rare that you can ever write down 'No one else is doing this at the moment, so there is no competition.' Even if you invent a revolutionary way to get the average consumer to the moon for a holiday and are the only company to be doing that, you'll still be competing with round-the-world cruises, road trips across America, and other holidays of a lifetime.

So, you've identified a customer, their needs and the competition they'll measure you against.

But these are all just theories, and we need to find a way to test them before going much further. If your theories are right, then your target customer will be willing to make some kind of commitment.

We're going to plan an experiment to see whether that will happen.

Do you remember back in Week Four when I said that the most important characteristic of an entrepreneur is a thirst for learning? Well, here's one of the key places that it can come into action.

Normal people would want to test their ideas and just get a good pat on the back and a lot of praise for how clever they are for thinking of it. You, as a true entrepreneur, aren't going to look for that. Not while I'm here to nag you anyway! You're going to look for what you can learn that will make your idea better, so you can better serve the customer.

This is an experiment. Things will go wrong – and that's what you want. The more you can road-test your idea and pick up on errors and criticisms, the better able you'll be to iron out the kinks and develop the idea into a winning proposition. So rather than be disheartened by (or worse, ignore) mistakes and criticism, embrace them. At this stage they are invaluable as a way to learn things from this experiment.

We're talking here about a very simplified version of an approach that entrepreneur Eric Ries calls 'The Lean Startup'. He believes that the principles of Lean management, which big industry uses to be as efficient as possible and to keep improving, can be applied to start-ups too. Among the ideas he puts forward are that you should experiment with your ideas as early as possible when failure is cheap, and keep improving them before you take them to market properly and failure is expensive. I've recommended his book at the end of this week if you'd like to explore these ideas in more detail.

Designing the experiment

Do you remember doing science experiments at school? You'd set out a theory or hypothesis, list the assumptions that underpin it, describe the method you will use in the experiment, list any apparatus/equipment/requirements, describe what happened – the results – and then write your conclusions.

We're going to do a very similar thing in the way we create an experiment to test your idea.

Hypothesis

This is where you make a sweeping claim about your idea that we are going to test with this experiment, such as 'I believe that pub customers in the UK will pay for a low-alcohol beer that tastes good' (I'm going to keep bringing this one up until somebody does it!).

Assumptions

Here you simply list the assumptions you have made implicitly in the hypothesis, and that need to be tested. So, for example:

A. 20 per cent of customers in pubs don't want to drink alcohol (at this stage, that's a guess).

B. These customers are not satisfied with current soft drinks because they are too sweet.

C. These customers are not satisfied with current low-alcohol beers because they taste bad.

D. If a customer is offered a new low-alcohol beer, they will be willing to pay to try it.

E. Beer drinkers in the UK will like the low-alcohol beer that we can import from Scandinavia.

Method

In this section you simply describe the steps you're going to take to val-idate each of the assumptions. I'll list them all here in this one method for simplicity. So what could you do in this case? How about these for some ideas:

1. To test [A], we will spend one evening sitting at the bar in three different pubs in town over the next week. We will keep a discreet record, just with ticks in different columns, of whether each drink we see being sold over the bar is alcoholic or not.

2. To test [A], [B] and [C], we will conduct a survey in these pubs, asking people how often they have nights out on which they don't drink alcohol, why that would be, what drinks they have then, and what they think of them.

3. To test [D], we will arrange with the landlord of our local pub, or the bar at some local event, to conduct the experiment, maybe even agreeing to help out behind the bar for free in return. We will put out some simply printed A4 laminated notices on the bar that say 'New! Tasty, refreshing low-alcohol beer – imported from Scandinavia. Tastes great, try it today, £3 a bottle.' We'll still do this, even if we haven't been able to import or brew any of the beer yet, and when someone orders it we'll just make a note, apologise that we've sold out and offer them something else.

4. To test [E], we will need to import some of the low-alcohol beer – maybe a friend could bring some back in their suitcase. We could organise a blind taste test of similar-style beers for our friends, with this one in among the selection, and get people to score them for various things such as taste, colour, how refreshing they are, lightness, etc. We won't mention that one is a low-alcohol beer until the end, then see if people are surprised. Finally, we will ask them if they'd ever buy our beer if they weren't drinking alcohol for the night. We could even ask if people want to place orders for some to see if they really did like it.

The key at this stage is the simplest validation of your assumptions that's possible. Keep it cheap and quick. Here are some examples of how entrepreneurs test their ideas in this way:

- If they're launching a web-based service or product, they create a really simple web page that explains what they will be launching and its benefits, and ask visitors to sign up to be among the first to access it when it's ready by entering their email address. People are very cautious about giving out their email address because of the spam problem, so it's an indication of their interest, even if they're not parting with money yet.

- If it's possible to make samples of your products, then take a stall at a car-boot fair, local market or other event and try to actually sell some. This is what the founders of Innocent Drinks did. They made a batch of smoothies in their home kitchen, took them to a music festival and sold them. They asked customers who'd tried them to put their empty bottle in different bins depending on whether the customer thought they should give up their day jobs to make these smoothies full time. At the end of the day, the 'yes' bin was full, and the rest is history.

- Surveys can be useful, but you have to put a lot of consideration into what you ask. It's very easy to lead people into the answer you want them to give, and that's no way to learn.

- Actually try to get orders for the product or service, even if it's only a glint in your eye at the moment. Once you have the order, apologise that you're out of stock (or even be honest and explain you're testing the market), say you'll be in touch when you're ready and give them a little something to make it up to them.

Requirements

Here you just list the things you're going to need to organise to conduct the experiment, such as:

- Arrangement with local pub or bar at an event.

- Some free evenings.

- A survey.

- Some printed notices.

- Some sample beer if possible.

This is then a To Do list for you, in order to be able to run the tests.

Get everything prepared and planned, so that you can do the experiments next week. If the planning takes a little longer, don't worry, it's worth it. Simply pick up next week when you're ready.

Emma

Emma's hypothesis is that office workers would like to buy healthier lunches if they were as quick to get as other lunch options, cost about the same, and were as filling.

To test the idea, Emma and Alan devise an experiment, in the way outlined above.

They agree that they'll ask a manager at work if they can bring in some salads for a week to sell to raise money for charity. They decide to ask Alan's manager, because no one in that department knows Emma well so there'll be less bias, and Alan won't say that he's involved. They'll both get up early and prepare the salads together before work, store them in a fridge in the office and Emma will come along and sell them at lunchtime – by asking for a donation to charity for each salad 'bought'. Alan will then listen for feedback. They'll develop three recipe ideas to try.

THIS WEEK'S TO DO LIST

- ☐ Write a paragraph or two about the target customers for your idea.

- ☐ Write down the needs and desires of your customer when it comes to your idea.

- ☐ Design an experiment to test your idea.

- ☐ Plan to carry out your experiment next week.

THIS WEEK'S RECOMMENDED READING

The Lean Startup, by Eric Ries (Portfolio Penguin).

The New Business Road Test, by John Mullins (Financial Times Prentice Hall).

An excellent book to help you refine and assess your business ideas.

8 Week Eight:
Testing and Refining the Opportunity

This week you'll be conducting the experiments you planned last week to test your idea, and then you'll refine it into an opportunity.

Learning from your experiments

Now that you've carried out your experiments, it's time to look at what happened and analyse what conclusions you can draw. Then you can see if you can improve your ideas.

Results

When it comes to writing up the result of your experiments, it's important to do it objectively. It can be so tempting to focus on the good news and quietly brush some of the awkward truths under the carpet. Remember what I said about learning? So, being honest, what did your experiments find?

In the example I gave you, let's say the results were as follows:

1. Only an average of 12 per cent of the drinks sold in the bars were alcohol-free or low alcohol.

2. The survey found that about half the people don't tend to have nights out where they don't drink at all – they just drink less if they have to drive or be up early, and make that one or two drink allowance last. The remaining half did tend to have alcohol-free nights and drank juice, lemonade and lime or similar soft drinks.

It did find that most people didn't really like drinking soft drinks in pubs because they're sweet, and pretty much the same price as a beer. Nobody currently knew of a low-alcohol beer they liked. In fact many people pulled funny faces at the thought.

3. Only three people asked for a bottle of the advertised low-alcohol beer.

4. At the blind tasting, all of the lagers on test got a reasonably good review except one, which was actually a fairly well-known brand of cheap lager. Everyone was surprised when it was revealed that one of the beers was low-alcohol. One of the guests asked to buy a case of it for a party they're holding the following weekend. Others said they would buy it if they saw it in bars now they knew it existed.

Conclusions

From the results you can then draw some conclusions. This is worth taking some time over and looking at the results from a different angle. Remember, this is all about what you can learn from the results to make your idea better and improve the experiments to learn even more next time.

In the example, you might conclude:

- Low-alcohol beer in the UK has a really bad reputation and people automatically think it's going to be horrible.

- People do have nights out when they don't (or shouldn't) drink alcohol, but the lack of savoury drink options means they either restrict themselves to a smaller number of alcoholic drinks, or drink juices etc.

- People do like the taste of the imported low-alcohol beer if they actually try it, and would then be prepared to buy it.

- Therefore education and tastings are going to be vital to the success of this idea.

- It's going to require either a large marketing budget to launch the business, or a planned slow rate of growth fuelled by tastings and word of mouth.

Refining or rejecting your idea

You've learned some really valuable things in a few simple experiments. So now's the time to fold those insights back into the original idea and improve it.

When considering how to refine your idea or whether to reject it, you need to bear in mind that:

- Feedback about one thing may be a symptom of another. For example, if people say 'it's too expensive' that doesn't necessarily mean the right response is to change the price. Maybe you need to improve how you explain the benefits and the value of your offer.

- Are you getting the feedback from the right people? If your target market is busy executives, feedback from friends who are students won't have much weight.

- People don't always know what they want, particularly if it's something innovative. Market research for the first photocopiers showed there was going to be very little customer demand – because people already had carbon paper! However, convincing them of something new is expensive – do you have that kind of marketing budget?

If, after considering all the above, you feel the feedback shows really clearly that the idea – however good it is – can't be made into an opportunity, then accept that. Reject it, and look for the next one. Entrepreneurs are ideas machines, and you'll soon find some inspiration for the next idea that could just become a big opportunity.

There's no hard and fast rule here – being an entrepreneur means you often need to rely on your gut feel. The key is to be really honest with yourself when assessing the result of your experiments.

Devising the next experiment

As you refine and improve your idea, you can also refine and improve the experiments in order to give you better insights, better data, and to learn as much as possible about what it'll take to make your idea an opportunity.

When you've really honed your idea into something you are sure is an opportunity that can become a profitable business, then it's time to move on to next week. It doesn't matter if this process takes you more than a week, it's worth the time.

Your business: a living experiment

This kind of exercise isn't just for the early stages of start-up. It's worth using this as a tool for continuous innovation in your business, even once it's highly successful. There are always things you can improve, new products or services you can launch, new markets to enter – and this simple approach to running experiments can help you do that in a cost-effective and flexible way.

Emma

Emma and Alan's experiment goes really badly on the first day and they only sell one salad. Alan asks his colleagues about it that afternoon and it turns out that most of them hadn't read the email he'd sent round about it and didn't know the option was there. So Emma suggests they put up some posters in the kitchen area and a leaflet on each person's desk. The next day they sell all twenty salads that they had made and raise £80 for charity. The feedback about the recipes is good, but there are quite a few people who don't like one of the ingredients in each salad, so they make a note that in future they'll probably have to offer a 'custom' option for fussy eaters. Some people were surprised at the addition of fruit and seeds, but after being persuaded to try it they liked them – so Emma and Alan realise that some of their marketing will need to do that persuasion for them.

They also learn that location is an important factor. By the end of the week some people are buying from them for the third time because 'it's so convenient'.

Emma and Alan have made lots of notes and spend the weekend assessing all the feedback they've had and devising some more experiments.

Overall, they think there's something in their idea.

THIS WEEK'S TO DO LIST

- ☐ Carry out your experiments.
- ☐ Write up the results.
- ☐ Think carefully about what conclusions you can reach and write them up.
- ☐ Refine or reject the idea.
- ☐ Improve the experiment and run it again.

THIS WEEK'S RECOMMENDED READING

Losing My Virginity, by Richard Branson (Virgin Books).

Branson is the master of testing out ideas and constantly improving them based on customer feedback or other circumstances. He started out with a student magazine and realised that people were making money from selling goods via mail order in the magazine, so he started selling records via mail order. Then there was a postal strike so he opened a shop people could go to to buy the records, and found that customers liked that experience and being able to listen to the music before buying, so he started opening more record shops. From being at the customer end of the music business he also realised that the record companies didn't really understand the music the young generation wanted – so he started a record label, and so on and so on. Many of his business ideas haven't worked out – including his sandwich delivery vans business (!) – but he keeps on experimenting.

9 Week Nine:
Pitching your Opportunity

This week you'll work at communicating the opportunity you've found.

Communicating your idea

Over the last few weeks you've developed your business idea and worked hard at researching and improving it until you believe there's a clear opportunity to build a profitable business from it.

This week you're going to start telling the world about your idea and learning how best to communicate it.

Start by writing roughly one page explaining:

● What your business will do.

● Who is it for (i.e. who will buy).

● Why they will buy.

● How the customers will benefit as a result.

● And summarising the research you have done to support this.

You may need to rewrite this a couple of times to get it right. Each time, read it through as if you were a complete stranger. Would you understand it? Would it excite you? If you answer no to either of these questions, rewrite it again. Emma's page is too long to reproduce here, but you can find it on the website.

START YOUR BUSINESS WEEK BY WEEK

Once you have a good page about your idea, try to write just one short paragraph that communicates the most important parts of your one-page document. Again, you'll need to rewrite this quite a few times until it's right.

Finally, write just one sentence about your idea. This is really, really hard to do well. You'll probably need to spend a lot of time on this to make sure it communicates as much as possible about your business idea in an exciting way in just one sentence. Later on this could perhaps be adapted to become the slogan of your business – being displayed below your company name to explain what you do. Picture it on your letters, on the front of a shop, on your company vehicles, on your adverts.

Emma

Emma's paragraph says:

> *'Leeds has a thriving financial services sector, bringing a lot of highly paid professionals to the city centre during the day. Many of these people are health conscious and are members of a gym or are following a diet, but at lunch they don't get a proper, nutritious, light meal – they end up eating fast food, or even nothing. My business will provide them with convenient, fast, healthy and tasty food. Our variety, quality and service will allow us to command a premium price.'*

For her sentence, Emma comes up with:

> *'My business will provide busy office workers with a healthy alternative for a fast, tasty lunch.'*

Or even shorter (good for using as her company slogan):

> *'Fast, healthy lunches for busy people.'*

Test your pitch on yourself

Before you take your idea to the world, test your pitch. Take an hour and find a quiet place in the house where you can think clearly.

First, read that single sentence out loud. Then answer these questions honestly:

- From just this sentence, do you understand what your company will do, who for, and what benefits it will bring them?

- Does the sentence make you, as the entrepreneur behind it, excited about the idea? Do you feel a 'buzz'?

If you answered 'Yes' to both of these, great – move on. If you answered 'No' or weren't really sure, then you need to work on rewriting that sentence. Remember you need to communicate what you will do, for whom and how that will benefit them.

Now review the paragraph you wrote, applying similar tests, and then do the same with the single-page summary.

Once you're completely happy with what you've written, it's time to go and try it out on other people.

A word of caution

If your idea depends on some kind of innovation or invention, which is the exception rather than the rule in business, you may be able to patent this. Patents are a form of legal protection for your idea and are only granted if your idea is not already in the public domain. If you think you will patent your idea, you can't go around telling everyone about it. You may want to put confidentiality agreements (otherwise known as Non-Disclosure Agreements or NDAs) in place in this case. For more information ask your mentor or local business advice centre.

Make sure you have a very good reason to ask someone to sign an NDA. If you don't it'll mark you out as an amateur – novice business people think that the idea is everything; experienced business people know that it's the execution, or the actions you take to make the idea work, that really matter, and people can't copy that.

Telling other people about your idea

This is a delicate moment in the evolution of any business – letting other people see your baby for the first time. Tell your family, your friends, your neighbours, your mentors, your colleagues. The more, the better – you want as much feedback as you can get. However, always remember that the results from your experiment are likely to be more valid than just people saying what they think. Actions always speak louder than words. Also, this is more about refining how you communicate your idea than what the idea actually is.

You'll get five types of feedback:

1. Negative with no good reason. This is bad, and it's always sad that some people are like this. They're sometimes called 'Neg-Heads' because they have such a negative mindset. They're really just scared of you becoming more successful than them, particularly if you've had exactly the same start in life.

2. Negative with good reason. This is the most valuable feedback it is possible to get. It is the only kind of feedback that will really help you improve your business and avoid potential problems. Thank these people from the bottom of your heart!

3. Neutral. Hmmm. This is bad. There's nothing they think you can improve, yet they're not very excited by your idea either. If you get a lot of this, then really examine your idea or the way you're communicating it very carefully. Maybe conduct some experiments with different ways of communicating it.

4. Positive with good reason. This is good as it's valuable to know exactly what people like about your idea. You could be on to a winner.

5. Positive with no good reason. This isn't very useful at all. The people who give you this kind of feedback, such as your gran, do it because they love you and want to say nice things about your ideas, but it doesn't help you build a successful business.

Whenever you get feedback from someone, jot down some notes. When you get back home, divide up their comments and categorise them under the above five headings.

You shouldn't let the Neg-Head comments get to you, so I've prepared a Neg-Head Bingo card for you. Scan through the comments that you are likely to hear and be ready for them. As you hear them, tick them off. If you get half the card or more, give yourself a small treat as a prize. If you get a full house, go out for a slap-up meal. It's best not to shout 'Bingo' as a Neg-Head says the last remaining comment on the card – they'll think you're even more odd.

NEG-HEAD BINGO			
If it really is such good idea, Big Company X would already be doing it.	It'll never work.	So you're the next Richard Branson/ Anita Roddick are you?	I once knew someone who started their own business, and he lost everything he had.
All right Del-Boy? This time next year you'll be a millionaire! (much laughter at their own joke).	What do you know about business?	It's far too risky! Why not get/keep a proper job?	Fancy the easy life do you? Giving up the 9 to 5 and working when you like?
What if it all goes wrong?	Where will you get the money?	You can't be a rich entrepreneur! You're from X	You'll be back here within six months wanting your job back.

Don't be tempted to categorise all criticism as Neg-Head though. Before you tick them off your bingo card and chuckle to yourself as you think about what your prize will be, give them real consideration. Why isn't Big Company X already doing this? Is it really because they are so big and slow that they haven't yet seen the opportunity, or is it because there's no money in it? Be honest with yourself. It may well be a negative comment with good reason.

Make a note of *all* the feedback you receive, in all categories.

Improving the way you communicate your idea

Now that you've received a lot of feedback, it's time to sit down and review it and see how the way you communicate your idea can be improved. (Notice how I didn't say 'if' there? It's 99.99 per cent likely that you will 'tweak' the way you pitch your ideas and improve them many times in the next few months. This is a good thing.)

Common problems you may need to fix are as follows.

- Your idea is too complicated. The simpler the idea, the better. In most cases potential customers don't have the time or the specialist knowledge to understand complicated new products or services.

- You haven't properly understood the needs of your target customer. While they may want the most exclusive, stylish product available, you may be offering the cheapest most unfashionable one – or vice versa.

- You haven't communicated your expertise or done enough to convince people that you'll be really good at what you plan to do.

- You haven't identified or communicated the most important benefits to the customer. What is it about your product or service that will convince them to part with their hard-earned money?

- You've left out the love, meaning there is nothing to distinguish you from bigger competitors.

Take some time to sit and read through the notes from the feedback you received and really give them some consideration. Consider also the common problems above. What can you do to improve your idea?

Then you'll need to rewrite your pitches to reflect the improvements you've made. Now go out drinking with your friends again and test your refined idea. Repeat until satisfied.

Shared Experiences

Trenton Moss, founder of Webcredible:

'I tested my idea by talking to everybody about it – absolutely anyone I could find. A lot of people tell you stuff you've already heard, or that's not really useful, but you just have to sit there and nod and wait, because often, after they've been talking for a while they'll come up with some piece of advice or an idea that proves incredibly useful.'

THIS WEEK'S TO DO LIST

- ☐ Write one page communicating what your business idea is.
- ☐ Write one paragraph that clearly summarises this.
- ☐ Write one sentence that is a simple pitch for the idea.
- ☐ Test and refine what you've written.
- ☐ Survive the Neg-Heads!
- ☐ Remember to update your weekly blog at **www.weekbyweek. net/startyourbusiness**

THIS WEEK'S RECOMMENDED READING

Brilliant Communication Skills, by Gill Hasson (Pearson).

The Pitching Bible, by Paul Boross (CGW Publishing).

10 Week Ten:
Customers

This week you'll work out more about your target customers, seeking to understand them and their industry – and what motivates them.

You've already done some work to understand your target customers as part of the experiments you've done. This week you're going to build up a really clear picture of who your customers are, how you will reach them, and why they will buy from you.

Who are your customers?

It's a good idea to develop a really strong picture of who your customers are. One way to do this is to create some fictional 'personas' that describe a typical section of your customer base. It's best to try to create between three and five of these personas.

So, for each one:

- Give them a name.

- Give them a gender.

- Give them an age.

- See if you can find a representative picture on the internet so that you can put a face to the name.

- Describe their lives/loves/hates/hobbies/values etc.

- Describe what their needs are.

Be as imaginative as you like with this exercise. Really try to picture each person as if they were a friend of yours. In future you'll even be able to refer to them in meetings – 'What would Andy think of this?' and so on – to help you to understand the impact of any idea on that customer segment.

If your target clients are other businesses, then imagine the people at those businesses that you'll be selling to.

Why will they buy from you?

Now you're starting to get to know these people, try to see things from their perspective. What are they looking for? What problems do they have? What factors will they take into account when making a buying decision?

Add all these details to their personas. You should then use these personas throughout your business planning and then in the future running of your business. Each key business decision can then be discussed by asking 'How would Anne feel about this?' or 'Will this new feature be useful to Andy?' and so on. You'd be amazed how real these personas can become in time and how helpful they can be in developing your business to better suit your target customers.

Emma

Emma and Alan write up their personas. They're based largely on merging people they know at work into certain categories. So there's one called Debbie, who's in her late forties and is trying to lose weight, so wants some healthier food. There's one called Kate, who's in her late twenties and tries to follow a healthy and ethical lifestyle – doing yoga, buying organic etc. – and would love to have somewhere to buy lunch that isn't a big chain, is healthy and also creative. 'Ed' is in his early thirties and a bit sceptical about salad. He thinks it won't fill him up and that he'll be hungry again by mid-afternoon. He's the customer they have to try to convince.

What type of business are you?

It's also important to understand where you fit as a business in the marketplace. There are two overall types of business, defined by who you're selling to. Will you be selling to businesses or individual consumers?

If you'll be selling to businesses, you're a B2B – business to business – company.

If you'll be selling to consumers, you're a B2C – business to consumer – company.

Then there are secondary types of business, defined by what you do for your customer. These are:

● Retail. You gather together a selection of products for your customers to buy via a catalogue, shop, website, stall at an event etc. In B2C you could be a clothes shop or a café. In B2B you might be an office supplies company.

● Manufacturing. You make things for your customers. In B2B you could be making car parts that you sell to a car company. In B2C you could be making handcrafted furniture.

● Service. You use your skills to provide a specialist service to your customers. In B2B you might provide office cleaning services or recruitment. In B2C you could be a plumber or a wedding planner.

● Knowledge. You provide your experience and knowledge to your clients, giving them advice or using your skills to work for them on short specialist projects. In B2B you could be a management consultant or an IT specialist. In B2C you could be a lawyer or a financial adviser.

Your company can be in more than one of these secondary types of business, so you could be a manufacturing company that also provides an ongoing service to the companies which buy the machines you make.

What industry are you in?

This is a fairly straightforward question to answer, and could be something like the catering industry, the rail industry, the fashion industry, the publishing industry, the car industry and so on.

What marketplace are you going to be operating in?

You may think that this is a really dumb question. It's obvious what marketplace you're in! The same as your industry!

Think of this question as being more 'What market are you in from your customers' point of view?'

Here's some food for thought to show you what I mean:

The railway company that operates services between Edinburgh and London is certainly in the rail industry. But is that the competitive marketplace that its customers see it in? If they're not keen on its quality of service, will they instead choose a competing train service that runs between Wales and London? No, they'll look instead at going by air, on the coach or in their own car. That's who the train companies compete with. They generally don't compete with each other at all. Their management teams need to keep up to date with what the UK short-distance air operators are doing, with what's happening to petrol prices, with road congestion etc. in order to best run their businesses.

Parker Pens had always thought they were in the stationery business and were facing price pressures as more and more people used cheap ballpoints instead of classy pens. They took a look at their business and found that from their customers' point of view they were in the gift-ware business. People bought expensive, high-quality pens as presents. They were competing with watches, jewellery, perfumes and so on.

Are takeaway restaurants just competing with other takeaways? Or are they in a wider convenience food market that includes supermarket ready meals?

You see what I mean now, so what marketplace or marketplaces are you going to be operating in from your customers' point of view?

Emma

Our case study entrepreneur is planning to start a B2C retail company. She will be operating in the catering industry and competing in the office-worker-lunch, fast-food and health-food marketplaces.

Becoming an expert

In order to succeed in your business, you need to become an expert in your market(s). Good knowledge will alert you to new opportunities, cost savings, new suppliers, new potential customers, new products, new competitors and anything else that matters. Customers will trust you more, and you'll be able to reach better deals with suppliers.

This week you should spend some time learning about your industry. Of course, you may already be an expert and that's why you've chosen this industry. In this case you need to make sure you stay an expert. It will be a wise investment to spend an hour or two each week keeping up to date with your industry.

Some places to start your research:

- Search for key terms in your industry on internet search engines. This will take you in the direction of news websites for your line of work, the online versions of trade newspapers or magazines, online industry discussion forums, and the websites of your competitors, suppliers and potential customers.

- Subscribe to the trade newspapers or magazines for your chosen industry. You can find these on the internet or your local library will help you find suitable titles.

- Browse big bookshops, either real ones or those online, for titles that relate to your industry. There may be 'how to' guides or a biography of a leading figure in the business.

- Select a daily newspaper that is likely to give some coverage of your industry (clue: unlikely to be the *Sun* or the *Mirror*). Remember that it may not be immediately obvious what is relevant to your business. For example, Emma has spotted an article about a campaign for healthier school lunches in the local paper. Although not immediately relevant to her target market, she decides she could do a campaign about 'leading by example', and that parents should have healthier lunches too.

- Are there any events for your industry? Conferences? Trade shows? Trade association meetings? All of these events are valuable places to meet useful people and find out information. Go along to as many as you can in the early days of your business.

- Could you work for a similar business for a while? Perhaps as an evening or Saturday job? Ideally this should be out of your target area so they don't feel that you've conned them when you start up in competition. One entrepreneur who was starting her own high-class catering company used her holiday to go and work for free in a hotel in Vienna, learning how to make stunning canapés.

Start a file (either on paper or on your computer) with notes on your key findings, clippings from magazines etc.

Looking for customers

The most vital things you should be looking for in all this research are people you can help – customers.

If you're going to be a B2B company, you should keep your eyes peeled for:

- The big customers in your industry.
- Any new coverage of upcoming projects by potential customers.
- The most active distributors or resellers in your industry.
- Information on the person in each potential customer company who is responsible for buying your products or services – what are their contact details?

If you're going to be a B2C company, you should try to find:

- Events that your target customers gather at.
- The media that your target audience use.
- Places that have a high number of your target customers.

In all cases you need to find the answers to these questions about your target customers:

- Exactly what are their needs?
- Which of these are vital, and which are nice-to-haves?
- Who do they buy from at the moment?

- How much do they pay?

- What are their unfulfilled needs?

- How much would they pay for these needs to be served?

- What is the main thrust of competition between the existing suppliers to these customers? Is it price? Speed? Quality? Reliability? Technology?

Look your customer in the eyes

However much research you do, nothing can beat getting out to actually speak to your potential customers.

If you'll be a B2B, do whatever you can do to get any kind of meeting. Have a formal meeting, get ten minutes with them at a trade fair or networking event, go for lunch, take them for a pint after work, anything.

Once you have them in front of you, you need to remember that the main point is to listen to them, not to talk to them. Because you're excited about your business it's all too easy to switch into 'transmit' and spend half an hour telling someone about your great idea, rather than switching into 'receive' and gathering the information you need.

Ask them about the challenges in their business and their job, any exciting projects they're working on, what their existing suppliers are like, what's most important to them in the service their suppliers provide, and what most irritates them about current suppliers.

Another word of warning: don't be tempted to bitch about your competitors. It's not professional and it will make your potential customer feel uncomfortable, or even set them against you.

Gather whatever information you can on this first meeting, and then keep in touch from time to time. Email is good for this.

If you'll be a B2C, find some of your ideal target market and ask them questions about their needs, where they buy from now, what they like, what they hate and so on.

In Emma's case she decides to get chatting to other people in the sandwich shop queue whenever she can, and to ask her colleagues at work – who are, of course, some of her target customers.

Your business plan

Now, you may not have realised it, but last week – when you wrote that page about your business opportunity, and in Week Five when you wrote about the founders – you wrote the first two sections of your business plan. See, that wasn't so frightening was it?

This plan will be the route map for you in the early days and the thought you put into it now will pay off ten times over. Don't be tempted to ask someone else to do it – you have to be behind every word and every number in this plan. Bank managers are never impressed by business plans that an entrepreneur hands over which have clearly been written by their accountant, however glossy it is. They would far rather have a more basically presented plan that is truly your work. You should also remember that this plan is going to be more for your use than the bank manager's. Once your business is up and running, you should be consulting the plan weekly to see how you're doing and what you might need to change.

The business plan you'll prepare over the next few weeks will suit most start-up businesses but, if you're planning to start a larger business and are going to be looking for a lot of funding from day one, I highly recommend you also read and work through *The Definitive Business Plan* by Richard Stutely. Details of the book are in Week Twenty. It could also be a useful book for you to dip into and pick up ideas even if your business will be more modest.

Each week we'll tackle a different section of the plan, doing the research then writing it up at the end of the week. At the end of the whole process, in Week Twenty we'll draw it all together into a finished business plan.

Writing the 'Customers' section of your business plan

This week you'll write the second section. This section is the most important in the whole plan. If the customers aren't there, or they don't have a need for what you do, or they won't pay enough for it, then it doesn't matter how good everything else in your plan is, your business won't work. It all starts with a customer.

This section of your business plan should be between one and three pages long. Start by focusing on who your customers are. Set out some details of the personas you created.

Describe roughly how many of these kinds of people/companies are in your target area, who they buy from now, what they pay, what needs aren't being met and so on – with particular focus on *why* you think they will buy from you.

If you're a B2B company, you'll win top marks here if you can name specific potential customers who you've talked to, and identified real needs. It's even better if you can get some kind of commitment from them to try you out when you launch.

Shared Experiences

Simon Murdoch was running a UK software company that provided software to major book retailers. He had an entrepreneurial idea to pitch to his customers, but his plans didn't work out:

'The internet came along and we talked to a lot of our customers about whether they should be on the web selling books – we were very keen to get some of our customers to commission us to develop internet book-selling operations. Unfortunately for various reasons, the big guys at Waterstones and Dillons either didn't want to do it or chose to develop their internet services with other people so eventually I just decided that if none of the big guys are going to choose us we will do it ourselves and compete with them.'

So Simon started Bookpages, an online bookseller that he later sold to Amazon to create **Amazon.co.uk**, making him a multi-millionaire in the process.

THIS WEEK'S TO DO LIST

- ☐ Create personas to represent your target customers.

- ☐ Consider what type of business you are and which markets you are operating in from the point of view of your customers.

- ☐ Work out who your early customers could be, or develop profiles of your expected 'typical' customers.

- ☐ Research your potential customers.

- ☐ Write up the 'Customers' section of your business plan, summarising what you have found.

THIS WEEK'S RECOMMENDED READING

The Entrepreneur's Guide to Customer Development, by Brant Cooper and Patrick Vlaskovits (Cooper-Vlaskovits).

11 Week Eleven:
Competitors

This week you're going to research your competitors to see what you're up against in winning your target customers' business.

Let me start by saying that everyone has competitors in their marketplace. Even if you have a revolutionary product or service that no one else provides, you will have competition for a share of your customer's wallet and mind.

While you've been researching your industry and your marketplace, and your customers and your suppliers, you may well have heard about your potential competitors. You can also do some research on the internet to find others.

This week you're going to find out as much as you can about these competitors.

Start by making a competitors' file, either in a lever arch file or on your computer. Create a section for each competitor (remember that you are looking at your competitors from the point of view of your customers – your marketplace competitors). Write a short document for each competitor of everything you know so far: name, address, phone number, product range, biggest customers, perceptions of them in the industry, feedback you've heard, rumours you've heard etc.

If you've seen any articles about them in the trade or general press, then cut these out and include them in your file. Keep an eye out from now on for anything you can put in this file to increase your knowledge of the competition. One website I recommend is **www.duedil.com** (it stands for 'due diligence', which is a process used in big business to check out the health of another company). This will allow you to see all sorts of publicly accessible records of limited companies.

Try them out

If at all possible, buy something from each of your competitors to see what the experience is like. For larger items you might just try buying and then not complete the purchase, or just make an initial enquiry.

What kind of service do you get? How knowledgeable were they? What were their prices like? What is the quality of their product or service like? What different ways were open to you to buy from them (phone, in person, internet, catalogue etc.)? Which did you find easiest?

You need to be really open-minded and honest here. Don't just go in trying to see the bad things – try to see what they do well. That's the only way you'll learn from the experience.

Add these notes to your file, and get as many product brochures and sample products as you can.

Key questions

- Who is your biggest competitor (in terms of financial size)?
- Who is the biggest brand name of all your competitors?
- Who will be your closest rival (in terms of closeness to your target market, service offering etc.)?
- Which competitor do you most admire?

The answer may be the same for some or all of these questions.

What will these companies do when you enter their marketplace? Will they react at all? Will they compete with you on their price, their quality or their brand name? Will they cut prices to try to drive you out of business? What would you do if you were them?

Spend some time thinking about and answering these questions.

Comparing your businesses

Now compare your plans for your business with the way your competitors do business:

- What are the similarities and differences between your products or services?

- Where are you positioned in terms of pricing? (Lowest is not necessarily best, but if you're high in the marketplace you have to justify this in terms of quality, convenience or love.)

- How professional will you seem in comparison?

- Why would customers buy from you instead of them?

- Why might customers buy from them instead of you?

Write up everything you've learned this week about your competitors for your business plan.

Based on what you've learned from your competitors, you may well want to go back and improve your plans from previous weeks. It's a good sign if you do! If you don't, are you sure?

Write up the 'Competitors' section of your business plan from everything you've discovered this week.

Emma

Emma and Alan each have lunch at different places in the local area every day this week, and compare their notes. They discuss the price, attractiveness of the shop and the display, the menu, the queue, the quality of service, and anything that made the place stand out.

They find there are a lot of similarities. Most of the big chains are very similar to each other, and most of the independent sandwich bars are very similar.

They like the way Pret A Manger has facts about the food all over the place, and that they have lots of staff so you get served quickly even when it's busy – but they find the choice a bit limited. However, at least they have some healthy options.

One of the independent cafés is terrible, but two of the others are quite nice. But nothing quite fills the gap that Emma had imagined.

They write up their notes into a two-page section of their business plan.

Shared Experiences

Trenton Moss, founder of Webcredible:

'I spent a lot of time researching my competitors. Most of the time I found them through web search engines. There were lots of people doing a similar thing to me, so I then tried to find a slightly different edge on what they were doing and build my company on that unique angle to make sure I was different enough.'

THIS WEEK'S TO DO LIST

- ☐ Start a file on your competitors.
- ☐ Do as much research on them as possible.
- ☐ Try buying from them.
- ☐ Compare your business to theirs.
- ☐ Write up a document summarising what you know about your competitors which will go in your business plan.

12 Week Twelve:
Branding

This week you'll develop the vision and values of your business, as part of beginning to develop the name and image of the company.

Many people think that branding is just designing a pretty logo – but in reality that's only the *result* of the branding work. Before that you need to know what your company is for, as well as the principles it stands for. These are generally known as the vision and values.

The terms vision and values seem a bit naff because too many large companies trot out big posters with all sorts of rubbish on them, and then never actually run the business in that way. Stuff like 'We believe people are our greatest asset', followed by a massive round of redundancies.

You can be different. You're an entrepreneur. Be authentic: say what you mean – and do what you say.

The big vision

What is your big long-term dream for the company? Why does it exist? What is the big difference it is going to make in the world?

This is all about the focus for your company. It can really help if you can narrow down what you are doing to something you can be the best in the world at, or at least the best in your market.

So Emma decides that her company vision is: 'Providing the tastiest, healthiest, fast food in the world'.

Values

These are the principles or behaviours by which you'll run your business. It'll be the character that will distinguish your company from the competitors. A good approach to this is to choose between three and seven words that really sum up what you're going to be like as a company.

Emma settles on: Healthy, Tasty, Fast, Caring, Inspiring, Fun. These are the characteristics she wants her business to have.

If you think about it, these could inspire her in many more ways than just delivering the product. How can the business really live the 'caring' principle? That could affect how it recruits and manages staff, it could mean that leftover food gets distributed to the homeless, or it could mean the business only buys fair trade fruit. And the 'inspiring' value could prompt her to produce a little recipe booklet for how to make really tasty healthy food at home – or she could put inspirational quotations on the boxes the salads get packed in and so on.

Having a set of values that is in tune with your business, and used whenever there is a key decision to be made, can actually be very inspiring.

Company name

In the next few weeks you want to gather as many ideas for names for your business as possible. Start a list on your desk and add to it every day – no matter how silly an idea sounds at the time, write it down anyway. You'll be amazed how it will spark a new idea a week or so later – or how it will continue to rattle around your head if you don't get it out by writing it down. You can also ask friends or family to have their own brainstorm to help you out.

The name you're ideally looking for would be fitting for your vision and values.

Some starting points for finding a name for your business are as follows:

Something based on your name. Ford Motor Company, WH Smith, Marks and Spencer, Sainsbury's, Rolls-Royce and Harry Ramsden's Fish and Chips are well-known examples of this. When you're big this can really help you give your business a personal edge and distinguish you from the competition, but it can also make you seem like a small company when you start out. Will that matter to you?

A word not connected with your trade that you could make to mean something in your industry. Orange did this in the mobile phone industry, Amazon have done it with online retailing, Virgin have done it with … well, everything! This can be a particularly smart idea if you plan to build a very big business, because the company name isn't too tied to you or to any particular industry. Richard Branson's first enterprise was a record shop, but just think of the problems Virgin would have with selling credit cards or mobile phones now if they had started trading as Vinyl Sounds instead. Or the problems Amazon would have in becoming a global company selling CDs, DVDs and even toasters if Jeff Bezos had started his business as Bezos Books.

Something that highlights the benefits to your customers. Budget Rent-a-Car, easyJet, Prontaprint, Kwik-Fit and Comfort Inn, for example.

Something that is based around your trade but gives it some added atmosphere or emotions. Coffee Republic, Pizza Hut, PC World and The Body Shop are all examples of this.

Something based around the values of your business. Innocent Drinks, The Co-Operative Bank are examples of this.

Everyone spends a lot of time worrying about their business name, but the truth is that pretty much any name will work if you get the rest of the business right. There are lots of well-known, highly successful businesses whose company names would be rejected if they came up in most brainstorming sessions. But has it held them back from becoming big and successful brand names? No. Examples include Smeg, Amstrad, ASDA, IKEA, General Motors and IBM. Would a big-name branding agency have proudly revealed these names to a fee-paying client in this day and age? No, but they work fine for the companies in question.

A good brand is not about what the words mean now, it's about what you *make* them mean through the quality of your work and the experience you give your customers.

So, start some 'Green Light' brainstorming and look for inspiration everywhere, and in a couple of weeks you can make a decision. Don't feel you have to rush into it.

Emma

Emma comes up with these ideas: Emma's Kitchen, Fast Salads, Fast and Healthy, Salad Shack, Vitality, Vite-ality (*vite* is fast in French, but Emma decides most people will miss her clever pun), Dashing and Delicious, High Speed Health, Tomato, and Speedy Salads before coming up with a name she loves: Racing Greens.

Deciding on a name

When you do come to make a decision, here are some factors to help you choose:

- Does it fit with your vision and values?

- Are other similar companies already using the name? Searching online can help find this out.

- Is the web domain name available for this name?

Domain names

If you want to have a website or company email address, you'll want to register your own domain name to look more professional and to make it easier for your customers to find. You may even want to register more than one to account for plurals or spelling mistakes.

Make a list of the domain names you would like and then visit one of the registration websites listed in the contacts section on the next page to check if they are available and how much they will be to register.

Emma does a search online and is delighted to find that both **racing greens.com** and **racinggreens.co.uk** are available. She buys both of them on her credit card from a registrar in the US for $37.85 in total for two years of registration. That's only about £25 at the current exchange rate (and Alan is very pleased about that bit!). She also looks into registering **racinggreen.com** and **racingreen.com** but finds they're not available, though she decides that doesn't matter too much for the kind of business she is.

THIS WEEK'S TO DO LIST

- ☐ Write down your company's vision.

- ☐ Write down your company's values.

- ☐ Start brainstorming for company names, and keep doing this each week until you have one you like.

THIS WEEK'S RECOMMENDED READING

Never Mind the Sizzle... Where's the Sausage? Branding Based on Substance Not Spin, by David J. Taylor (Capstone).

The 22 Immutable Laws of Branding, by Al Ries and Laura Ries (Profile).

LIST OF CONTACTS

Domain registrars:

123-reg.co.uk
eNom.com
Gandi.net

13 Week Thirteen:
Sales

This week you'll think about how to persuade people to buy from you, and how you'll ensure they'll want to buy from you again in future.

You've identified who your early customers could be. For the next section of your business plan you need to answer the following questions, which are shown with some suggestions to set you thinking:

Where will your customers buy your products or services?

- From your premises.
- From their premises with you visiting them.
- Over the phone.
- From distributors or retailers.
- From partner companies.
- From your website.
- At home-shopping parties.
- At events such as conferences, trade shows, country fairs etc.

What will persuade them to try your products or services?

- Signage.
- Advertising.

- Publicity.

- Marketing materials.

- Word of mouth.

- Promotions.

- Free trials.

- Demonstrations.

- Your personal relationship with them.

- Your reputation in the industry.

- Your skills as a salesperson.

Why will they buy from you rather than your competitors?

How much will you charge for your products or services?

If this is more than your competition, why will your customer be prepared to pay a premium?

If this is less than your competition, why?

How have you arrived at your price?

Pricing is always difficult in any business. Most start-up entrepreneurs price their services too low because of a lack of self-belief or a misguided idea that it's only low price that matters. If you're providing a quality service, make sure you charge a quality price!

For now, estimate your pricing here based on your gut feel, and we'll revisit this later in the financial section of your plan (Week Eighteen).

How will you make sure they will buy from you again?

- Quality.

- Level of service.

- The love.

- Your services or products are unique.

- Special offers for repeat customers.

- Promotions.

Now you have some notes and ideas, write these up into a one- or two-page 'Sales' report for your business plan.

Emma

Emma and Alan decide they'll open a small shop to base themselves from, and agree that it will need to be near the office area of town rather than the shopping area. They also decide that they'll do deliveries to local offices, taking orders by email. Customers who sign up for this service will receive an email at the start of each day with the menu and a summary of the daily specials and can then just reply with their order. They pay in cash when their order is delivered.

Emma comes up with the idea that customers could subscribe to one of two services by paying in advance on their credit card, by cheque or in cash. The Racing Greens Club will give the customer a certain number of vouchers that they could use to pay with when their order is delivered. Whenever they run low on vouchers, they could buy more with their card. The Racing Greens Fast Track means that customers are billed at the start of each month for all lunches that month. When they first join they specify any likes, dislikes and allergies, and then they automatically receive a lunch each day. They can email by 10 a.m. each day to cancel that day's lunch (e.g. if they have to go to a business lunch), and it's credited to their account so that next month's payment is lower.

Alan turns white at the thought of all this administration, but really likes the overall idea and sees the potential for winning high customer loyalty. They decide to leave it until they have been up and running for six months, and have their first staff members, and then to launch the schemes as additional new services.

Alan is quick to realise that the fast way to success is by encouraging as many people as possible to try Racing Greens as soon as possible after opening day. He suggests some discount coupons, and they decide that to celebrate their opening day they will give out coupons offering a free lunch for a friend – a 'buy one, get one free' offer.

They also decide that they will actually have the official opening a week after the actual opening, and promote the first week as a 'preview'. They won't open to the public during this week, but will distribute VIP vouchers to members of local business clubs, key local decision-makers and so on, offering a half-price lunch during the preview week.

They decide that they will charge above the existing local market for takeaway lunches, as the quality and health benefits are so much higher.

THIS WEEK'S TO DO LIST

- ☐ Plan how you will persuade your target customers to buy from you.
- ☐ Write up the 'Sales' part of your business plan.

THIS WEEK'S RECOMMENDED READING

Sold! How to Make it Easy for People to Buy from You, by Steve Martin and Gary Colleran (Pearson).

14 Week Fourteen: Premises and Equipment

This week you'll begin arranging all the resources you're going to need for your business.

Starting a business is hugely exciting and it's easy to get carried away by the buzz. One of the areas I see this happen in most is when choosing premises and buying the equipment. Everyone goes out to get the Rolls-Royce version straight away, when really they could start with a Mini and only work their way up as the business can afford it.

It's really, really important to keep your cost base low. Do everything as cheaply and simply as possible – but that doesn't mean the customer has to see that it's cheap.

Premises

Do you really need premises for your business from the start?

Most businesses where the customer must come to you, such as cafés, restaurants, hairdressers and so on have no choice but to get premises from the start.

If you're a retailer, you may have decided that you need a shop rather than relying on catalogues, home-shopping parties, events or the web (which I do urge you to think seriously about, at least to try out your idea in the short term before committing yourself to expensive rents).

You need to first identify the area in which your shop should be located (you may have done this last week), now you need to keep your eyes peeled for shops to let. They may have signs outside or be advertised in the press. It's also worth calling in to some of the shops in that area and talking to the owners. Who do they rent from? Would they recommend them? Have they had any problems? Do they know of any properties coming on to the letting market soon?

If you're going to be manufacturing something, can you do this from yours or a friend's shed for a while on a small scale? If not, you'll probably need premises, but it's often unlikely that your customers will ever see where you're based, as you will tend to visit them to sell and deliver. That means you can look around for the cheapest rents. These will probably be in small rural trading parks. Drive around the market towns and villages in your area looking for them, look for adverts in your local newspaper, and talk to some of the local letting agents.

If you're going to be an office-based business, can you get away with working from home? Could you convert a spare room, a garage or a shed into your offices? If so, check the terms of your mortgage (or your tenant's agreement if you rent) and the deeds of your house to ensure you're not prohibited from doing so. You will also need to inform your home insurance company.

In my most recent business there were fifteen members of the team, and we *all* worked from our own homes. We were simply connected all day using a VoIP (Voice over Internet Protocol) phone service, online chat, email and so on, and would try to meet up as often as we could. It meant I could hire the best staff, wherever they happened to live.

Other options for premises are:

- **Business incubators**. These are small groups of office and light industrial units that are available to start-up business. They often come with a package of business advice and support to help you grow. Some are run by local government, others by universities, and the rest by the private sector. They all have different business models. Some simply provide cheap easy-in, easy-out premises for your business, others spend a lot of time and effort helping you grow. The latter often require you to give them an equity stake (shares) in your business in return. You can find them by searching on the web or through your local business link.

- **Sharing space**. Do you know anyone in business who could rent you a corner of their office, shop or factory very cheaply to help you out? If not, ask friends if they know anyone who could. I started my first business by simply renting one desk in the corner of another company's offices.

- **Serviced offices**. These are companies who buy or lease a building, divide it up into smaller offices and rent these out to small businesses or larger businesses who need a small local office in another town. They often provide a receptionist who can take your calls as well as fax and photocopy services. Contracts can be for relatively short periods so it's a good way of being able to test your idea.

Before you search for your premises, write a list of exactly what you need the premises to have. Think about the following: location, size, local facilities, security, parking and anything else that might be necessary for your business.

Next, contact commercial property agents (who may be estate agents or chartered surveyors), give them the list and ask them to send you details of suitable properties. Get the local paper and look for adverts for commercial property, search on the web and ask around. Find as many suitable premises as possible and then arrange viewings.

Things to ask when viewing premises:

- How much is the rent?

- Is the rent all-inclusive or are there any extra service charges?

- Does the rent include any utilities (see p.113)? Who are the current providers of these utilities?

- Is it the landlord or you who'll be responsible for the maintenance of the external structure of the building? (It's bad news if they say you are.)

- Is it the landlord or you who'll be responsible for the maintenance of the internal structure of the building? (This is likely to be you, unless it's a serviced office or incubator.)

- When do the premises become available for you to occupy?

- What will the current tenant or the landlord be taking away before you move in?

- How long is the minimum rental period?

- How long is the notice period?

- How often is the rent reviewed, and is there a formula for doing this?

- Are there any restrictions on the use of the property in the lease or rental agreement?

- What classes of use has the local planning authority approved the premises for?

- How much are the business rates for the premises currently?

- If the premises get on to your shortlist, would they mind your insurance broker visiting in order to prepare a quote for you?

- Have the premises ever been broken into?

- Will they give you a rent holiday on moving in, in order for you to spend the money on getting the premises ready for use? This is quite common, and you don't get if you don't ask.

- Will they give you a reduced rent payment on the first year to help you get going? Again, this is quite common, so don't be afraid to ask. For both these points they are likely to say no at first, but remember – negotiation and persistence are key skills for an entrepreneur.

- Do the premises have parking? Is it enough for your needs? Does this cost any extra?

Select your ideal premises, plus a few back-up options. Note down all the facts. Don't sign up to, or commit to, anything yet! Now write up a short summary of your options.

You may need to continue this search over the next few weeks, or even months, until you find the premises that are just right for you. It's best not to compromise as you'll only regret it later. You'll be better off delaying the start of your business to get big decisions like this right.

If you'll be working from home, you can get your business to pay you some rent on the part of your property that you use for work. This can be a tax-efficient way of getting some money out of the business, but you'll need to get some professional advice on this from your account-ant once you've selected one (covered next week).

Utilities

As noted above, you should find out whether the cost of your intended premises includes the bills for any of the utilities. Serviced offices and incubators often include most of the utilities.

Think about each of the following utilities:

- **Electricity**. How much will this cost a month? Most electricity companies will give you an estimate if you tell them the type of premises (or the address if possible) and the type of business you'll be running there.

- **Gas**. Does the heating/water system in your premises run on gas? Again, try and get an estimate of the monthly bills.

- **Water/sewage**. You'll have to pay this or keep your legs crossed all day. How much is it?

- **Council services**. You'll have to pay business rates (which are like council tax). There will also be separate charges for services such as dustbin collection. Find out from the agent or owner what these will be, or ask the council direct.

- **Telephone line**. You'll need to get at least one phone line installed (and broadband too). Is there a line already? Check if the line has been 'stopped', in which case the phone company will cheekily charge you £125 to 'reconnect' it, even though they just have to press a button on the computer! What will the other connection costs be?

Write a summary of what utilities you'll use from which suppliers, and how much this will cost.

Refurbishment costs

The premises you find might need some work on them before you can use them. Get an estimate for the cost of this.

Equipment

While you're looking for premises, you also need to work out what you'll need to run your business.

If you're going to be retailing, this will include display units, a counter, tills, lighting and credit card machines (more on credit card machines next week).

If you're going to be in food retailing or catering, you'll need all the equipment to prepare the food, fridges or chiller cabinets to store and/or display the food, a till, a credit card machine and a counter. If customers will be eating on your premises, you'll need tables, chairs, cutlery, crockery, trays and other items to serve the food.

If you're manufacturing, you'll need to find suitable machinery for your purpose. Try to find this second-hand if possible. Ask around your contacts, or search on the internet to find a suitable supplier.

Most businesses will need some kind of office equipment, including: desks, chairs, filing cabinets, shelves, noticeboards, computers, printers, desk lights, telephones, as well as a wireless access point if you didn't get one as part of your broadband plan. You might also need a vehicle of some kind.

Sit down and write a big list of every item you'll need, however small, using the short lists above as a starting point. Where can you get these for free or cheaply? Could people lend them to you, could you buy them second-hand? Remember, the mantra at this time is to keep it cheap!

Research potential suppliers and find rough estimates of how much this equipment might cost you.

You can search for suppliers locally in your Yellow Pages, in the trade press or in an online directory such as Kelly's (see the 'List of Contacts' section).

Emma

It's clear that Emma and Alan will need a shop from the start. They begin their search by walking around their local area after work one day and making notes of any empty shops.

They find one that was previously a café, in a spot that they think would be ideal. Alan is worried that if the previous owners couldn't make a café work here, then maybe they can't either – but Emma thinks that a sit-down café is the wrong offering in this area which is where office workers want to pick up quick lunches to take away. But they decide they'd better do some more research.

It's just three doors down from a big Pret A Manger branch, so people do definitely come here to get their lunches – and the shop front is quite visible as you walk along the street. The big advantage to it previously being used as a café is that they know they won't need to get any extra permissions to sell food from there.

There's a sign in the window for the agent that is handling the lease and after they've met him a few days later they find that the rent is higher than they'd expected. As the shop has been empty for a while because of the economic conditions, they get the feeling they'd be able to negotiate a little.

They put together details of the other things they'll need, contacting a local catering supplies company to get information on fridges, display cabinets and so on.

Shared Experiences

Richard O'Sullivan is the Managing Director of Millie's Cookies. They don't have flashy, expensive head offices:

'Because the business was built from the bottom up, because it started out as a one- and two-man operation, we have always controlled a very tight overhead. We would much prefer to put our cash into brilliant people and beautiful stores than posh offices. We don't generate any sales from offices – if we did we'd put a cash register there!'

THIS WEEK'S TO DO LIST

☐ Write down a list of what you need your premises to have.

☐ Search for premises via agents, in the press, by asking around and on foot/in your car.

☐ Arrange viewings at suitable premises and run through the checklist of questions above.

☐ Identify a shortlist of around three possible premises and write up your findings.

☐ Identify which utilities you will need and find out their costs. Write up your findings.

☐ Compile a list of all the equipment you'll need, where you could get it from and how much it will cost.

THIS WEEK'S RECOMMENDED READING

Start Small Finish Big, by Fred DeLuca with John P. Hayes (Warner Business Books).

How Subway grew from one sandwich shop to become a global brand – and great advice on how you can do the same. This includes descriptions of how Fred went about finding and negotiating on his stores.

LIST OF CONTACTS

Kelly's Directory: **www.kellys.co.uk** – an online directory of suppliers and their products.

The National Association of Estate Agents: **www.naea.org.uk** – search for an estate agent in your area.

The Royal Institution of Chartered Surveyors: **www.ricsfirms.co.uk** – ask/search for commercial property agencies for your area.

15 Week Fifteen:
People and Technology

> This week you'll continue work on pulling together all the resources you need to provide your service to your customer.

If you've decided to go down the route of finding premises for your business from the start, then last week was probably a very busy one, and you're likely to still have properties to view this week and perhaps for the next few weeks. That's fine – don't feel you have to rush it.

In the meantime, there's more work to do to plan your resources.

People

Is it at all possible that you could get away without any staff in the early days? If there's more than one of you starting the business this should be easier, but even if it's just you it's worth thinking about. Early on in the life of your business you're going to have to work your backside off, doing every little job under the sun, but you'll be keeping the expenses, and the risk, down.

In this book I'll assume that this is what you will do – after all we are just starting small at this stage.

If you really, really need other people from the start, then perhaps friends and family could help out at first and you could have a plan to recruit people after six months or a year.

In some businesses, though, you need to hire full-time staff from day one. If this is the case, then I have suggested some useful books and resources in the 'Recommended Reading' section at the end of this week. You can also find useful information on the website at **www.weekbyweek.net/startyourbusiness/week15**

How will you go about recruiting these people? Recruitment agencies can be expensive and generally aren't too impressive (with a few exceptions). Advertising for recruitment vacancies is also expensive. This is where you can use your networking contacts and put the word around, and get family and friends to spread the word. Perhaps you could put up notices in local sandwich shops that working people get their lunch in? Perhaps you could get a good news story in the local paper about a new business that's creating jobs? You could advertise online on Gumtree or other listings sites, or to your contacts on LinkedIn or Facebook. Think of all the ways you could be more creative in how you find the right people and write these down as part of your recruitment plan.

If there's one role that's vital for you to do personally at this stage it's the sales role. Only you have the passion for your business and the focus to serve your clients. Sales people you recruit will be more focused on what money they get than your long-term business goals and you'll just spend all your energy managing them. It's much easier to recruit good people to do the other tasks in the business and to have you as the face of the company for your customers.

If you're going to need staff than you'll need to get specialist advice from your accountant in a few weeks' time (which is when we'll be finding you one!).

Technology

Start-up businesses are gaining increasing power and competitiveness through the use of technology. Mobile phones, email and websites are all bringing the world to the entrepreneur – and taking the entrepreneur to the world. With fairly cheap technology you can do the same things as the big companies. How can you make this work for you in your business?

Computers

Will you need more computers than you have now? What about printers? These days I mainly use my printer for boarding passes and other tickets – everything else is just done electronically.

What sort of specification will you need on each computer? How much will it cost?

Software

What software will you need to run on your computers?

Most of what you need you can run in the browser these days using online services (which I'll go into next).

But you may decide you need software for word processing, spreadsheets or databases. Microsoft Office and **OpenOffice.org** are the main providers (with the advantage that OpenOffice is free, though it's not quite as easy to use).

Will you need any specialist software for your industry?

Online services

These days there is a huge range of useful services for entrepreneurs available online. Here are some I recommend considering.

Accounting

These services can help you keep track of your money and produce the necessary reports:

- www.freeagent.com
- www.freshbooks.com/uk
- www.kashflow.com
- www.xero.com

Additionally, the following online services can integrate with some of these accounting packages to add more functionality:

- **http://floatapp.com** – helps you forecast your cash flow
- **www.quoteroller.com** – helps you build sales proposals and quotes

CRM

Customer relationship management services help you keep track of your key customers and sales:

- **www.capsulecrm.com**
- **www.nutshell.com**
- **www.sugarcrm.com**

Point of sale

Provides a computer-based (or even iPad-based) alternative to a cash register:

- **www.vendhq.com**

General team and project management

Enables you and your team to collaborate and manage your projects:

- **https://podio.com**
- **http://basecamp.com**

Other team communication tools

Help you to stay in touch and keep information flowing around the company:

- **https://www.yammer.com**
- **http://status.net**
- **www.skype.com**

Email

There is a range of good email providers that offer a free service. I use Google's **gmail.com** (and their business version **google.com/apps** includes a free version for up to ten users and allows you to use your own domain name) because of the good user interface and the excellent spam filtering. Microsoft have recently launched **Outlook.com**, which I haven't yet tried.

Website

A website will almost certainly be important for you – even if it's just a place for customers to find out information about you.

You could create a simple brochure site or blog yourself using something like **Wordpress.com**. You can create something a little more advanced using **DrupalGardens.com**, but you'll need to be a bit more geeky.

You may decide to go further though and have an e-commerce-enabled website, allowing customers to buy your products online. **Shopify.com** allows you to do that very easily and cheaply.

But you might decide you need to hire someone else to build the site for you. Web design companies aren't cheap, so if you know someone who's technical, then ask them if they would help you. But if the website will be central to what you do, you may feel a more professional approach is needed.

To save money you can suggest that the web design company uses one of a range of open-source software packages I've listed below. These are free software packages, so you will only have to pay for the web designer's time in setting them up. Then you'll be able to update the site yourself using the software.

Get some quotes from local web design agencies and freelancers. You can also find designers in the forums sections of the websites connected with the open-source software packages. These people are ideal because they know the software really well.

Whoever you talk to, ask to see examples of their work – real sites, not just pictures of the screen. Try out the site. Is it fast? Does it look good? Is it easy to navigate?

Also, you'll want to make sure that they'll give you access to the content management system and make it easy for you to update or add content yourself, otherwise you'll end up paying for every update. Plus, make sure that it'll be easy to move the site to being managed by another provider in case you don't get on with the first one.

Remember that you're just getting quotations for now though (for both the initial design and build, as well as for any ongoing charges for hosting, support etc.), so don't commit to anything just yet.

Payment services

If you want to take payment over the internet, a starting point is to use an online service such as **Paypal.com** or **GoCardless.com**. You can also arrange a merchant services facility with your bank, which allows you to take credit cards directly on your website, but this can be expensive so is only really worth doing when you're a little bigger, or if you're absolutely sure you can afford it now.

At the same time you may also want to decide whether you will need to process credit card transactions offline, in the real world. Will you be selling face to face to the customers, or via the post? If you want to accept credit cards via these methods, you'll need to open a merchant services account. Speak to your bank manager and get some quotes – but be aware that you don't have to get your merchant services account from the same bank you have your main current account with.

Your provider will give you a terminal, like you see in restaurants and shops, for you to swipe the customer's card through and enter the amount they need to pay. The machine then connects via a telephone line to the bank, checks that the card is not stolen or over its limit, checks the PIN and authorises the transaction. The bank then takes the money from the customer's account, holds on to it for a few days or weeks (depending on the card-processing company) and then pays it into your account.

Telephones

Will you need more than one phone? Will you need a telephone switch (an automated switchboard) and multiple lines? You may be able to avoid the expense of a telephone switch by using a service from BT called Featureline. All your telephones plug into sockets on the wall that connect to the telephone exchange in the normal way, but you can dial between handsets for free, you can transfer calls, if one handset is engaged the exchange will try others until it gets through and so on – it's just like having a switchboard. You can have up to 60 handsets – which should be enough for you for now!

You could also use a VoIP telephone service, which delivers your calls over your broadband connection to a handset that plugs into your router. This provides you with the same facilities as a corporate switchboard at a much reduced price. In the 'List of Contacts' section there's a link to a provider I've used and been pleased with (I have no connection to them other than being a customer), but a quick search online for 'VoIP provider' will give you a lot of options.

Will a mobile phone be important in your business? If you'll need more than one, you can get business tariffs from all the leading providers that give you discounts on the package as a whole.

Broadband

Can you get away with a cheap consumer connection, or do you need a higher bandwidth professional connection with a lower contention ratio?

Writing the 'Resources' section of your business plan

You now have all the information you need to finish this section of your business plan. Pull together your notes from last week and this week, and summarise what resources you'll need in the business, why you will need them, where you'll get them from and what they will cost.

Emma

Alan investigates the accounting systems and decides on **Freeagent. com** as something simple that he can get to grips with. He also looks into purchasing a cash register.

They both decide that they'll staff the shop themselves for now, and only bring in help once it's up and running.

Emma looks into getting a website started and decides the easiest and cheapest thing to do for now is to build one on **Wordpress.com** with just a few pages of information about the shop, their salads and what makes them special. Later they can move to something more advanced if they think it's needed.

They decide to each get a cheap laptop that they can use for running the business.

Shared Experiences

Sahar Hashemi came up with an innovative recruitment technique for Coffee Republic when she found it difficult to find staff through traditional routes:

'We put an advert in the Evening Standard for staff, but the replies sounded just like the sort of people we didn't want and I had to think how else to do it. At the time we were very impressed by Pret A Manger staff, they were very smiley and uniformed etc., so our solution was to just go and nick them from Pret A Manger. We approached two people, offered them 50p more an hour and that's how we started employing staff.'

THIS WEEK'S TO DO LIST

- ☐ Identify whether you need to hire any more people– and, if so, get some extra advice on this at: **www.weekbyweek.net/startyourbusiness/week15**

- ☐ Identify what technology you're going to need.

- ☐ Research where you'll get that technology from and what it will cost.

- ☐ Write up the 'Resources' section of your business plan.

THIS WEEK'S RECOMMENDED READING

How to Build a Great Team and *Fast Thinking Manager's Manual*, 2nd edition, both by Ros Jay (both Pearson).

The latter is a very useful collection of short guides to key management issues – if you're hiring people that means you're about to become a manager! It includes three or four guides that are really useful for selecting new staff and helping them get started.

LIST OF CONTACTS

Orbtalk, a VoIP provider: **www.orbtalk.co.uk**

16 Week Sixteen:
Suppliers

This week you'll be identifying your needs for external suppliers and finding out what potential suppliers can offer you.

You've now pulled together everything that you're going to need to have inside your business – but that's still unlikely to be everything you need. This is where you will need to find external suppliers. These are the external businesses on which you will rely on a regular and ongoing basis to enable you to serve your customers (rather than the companies that will sell you things on a one-off basis, such as the start-up equipment we discussed last week).

Accountants would refer to the costs of the suppliers in the previous weeks as 'Overhead Costs', and the cost of these suppliers as 'Cost of Goods Sold' or 'Cost of Sales' because these are costs you incur each time you make a sale.

If you identified last week that you need staff in the early stages of your business, keep in mind during this week that you may be able to use an external supplier in the early stages instead.

Through your research into the industry and market that you're going to operate in, you should have a good idea of who the key suppliers are. Now write a list of all the products or services you'll need from them.

Here are some suggestions to get you started:

- **Retailer**. The products for you to sell, or courier services if you plan to sell by mail order or the web, even luxury carrier bags and giftwrap. If you'll be selling food, you'll need food and drink, packaging, cutlery, napkins, condiments etc.

- **Manufacturer**. The raw materials you need to make your products, the packaging to put them in and the cost of delivering them to the customer.

- **Knowledge-based business**. You'll have very few items under 'Cost of Goods Sold', because you're essentially just selling the use of your brain for a period of time. You may want to sub-contract to other consultants though, or you may sell to your clients products or services that you buy from elsewhere. For example, a software consultant might research the market for a client, decide on the best software, buy it and then add a mark-up before billing the client or take a commission from the software supplier.

- **Service**. You may have the cost of products that you need in order to provide the service, spare parts etc.

Getting information

Now you have a list of what you need, approach potential suppliers to get more information and a quote. You can find potential suppliers in the same way you did in the 'Equipment' section of Week Fourteen.

In order to prepare a quote for you, suppliers are likely to need to know:

- Exactly what products you need.

- How many you will want to order each time.

- How often you might be ordering.

But many suppliers should just be able to send you a price list.

Understanding pricing

Suppliers may give their prices in any of the following ways:

- **Simple price**. What you see is what you pay. This is generally used by businesses selling to other businesses, where you will then do a lot of work on the product and the original product will be a small part of a bigger whole once you sell it on to your end customer. For example, if you're making cars and are buying rubber hose, you will just pay a price per metre.

- **Recommended retail price, less trade discount**. This is generally used by suppliers to the retail and service trade, where the goods are going to be sold on unchanged to the end user. For example, if you run a bookshop, you'll buy the books from the publisher at around 40–50 per cent discount off the recommended retail price.

- **Simple trade pricing**. There will be a simple trade price listed. That's the one you pay.

You'll want to ask them:

- To send you a catalogue and any other supporting information.

- What the procedure is for opening an account with them and if they can send you the forms. (Hold on to these when they arrive, we'll fill them in in Week Twenty-One.)

- What their credit terms are. (30 days' credit is fairly standard, but they may require payment up front for the first order, then 30 days. Try to get the credit period for as long as you can.)

- How long it will take them to deliver once you've placed your order. (This is known as the 'lead time'.)

- What their returns policy is if you find a product to be faulty or incorrectly supplied.

- If VAT is charged on their products/services. (We'll cover VAT in Week Twenty-One.)

- What after-sales service or support is available. (This is particularly important if the product is hi-tech!)

- If they can put you in touch with anyone else they supply for you to get a reference about them.

- What marketing support they can provide. Leaflets? Posters? Displays? Advertising support?

- If they can send you samples for you to check that they're suitable for your needs and of good quality.

Remember, a key skill of entrepreneurs is negotiation. Use it! Always try to get more, or get it cheaper, or get longer payment terms.

Payment terms are one of the most difficult things to negotiate with suppliers as a start-up business. Suppliers are often reluctant to give you any credit because they're worried about you going out of business. Many will want to be paid cash up front for at least the first order. Try to get to know the owners or managers of your key suppliers and build up a personal relationship to try to avoid this.

It's going to be quite some time before you place your first order with them, but it's really worth establishing these contacts and relationships now in order to avoid delays or disappointments later.

Writing the 'Suppliers' section of your business plan

Now write up a short report for your business plan on the list of suppliers you plan to use, what they'll supply you with, on what terms and at what price.

It's useful to identify back-up suppliers in case you have any problems with your first choice.

Emma

Emma visits a local gastropub where she's eaten a few times with friends and they know her face, and asks if they would mind telling her about their suppliers. When it gets to a quiet period the chef comes out with a list and talks her through the local wholesalers – who sells what, who is good for each type of ingredient, and what kind of terms they give including minimum order value. They talk about how often she should place orders and how to estimate how much to order, as well as how to manage the stock once it arrives.

In the next day's lunch break she phones round the people on the list and gets them to send her details and account opening forms.

Shared Experiences

Your relationship with suppliers is about more than just price, they can help your business in many other ways. Barry Gibbons is now involved in a number of entrepreneurial companies, but recounts an experience from when he was Chief Executive of Burger King in the early 1990s:

'We took a decision early on to move from Pepsi to Coca-Cola as our drinks supplier. Pepsi was cheaper but Coke offered a more comprehensive partnership: investment in equipment, support and service, and a marketing partnership.'

THIS WEEK'S TO DO LIST

☐ Write a list of everything you need to source from an outside supplier.

☐ Identify suitable suppliers.

☐ Contact them to find out details of their product or service, pricing, terms and other information.

☐ Write up the 'Suppliers' section of your business plan.

☐ You're going to need these leaflets and forms from HMRC (the people who administer VAT) in a couple of weeks, so order them now:

    i. Form VAT 1: Value Added Tax (VAT) – 'Application for registration';

    ii. Notice 700: 'The VAT guide';

    iii. Notice 700/1: 'Should I be registered for VAT?';

iv. Notice 700/21: 'Keeping VAT records';

v. Notice 731: 'Cash accounting';

vi. Notice 732: 'Annual accounting';

vii. Notice 733: 'Flat rate scheme for small businesses';

viii. and, if you'll be in retailing, Notice 727: 'Retail schemes'.

HMRC's contact details are below.

LIST OF CONTACTS

HMRC: **www.hmrc.gov.uk**

The organisation that administers the Value Added Tax scheme (VAT). They are very helpful and their forms are very clearly designed and simple to understand. I give them full marks for their efforts in trying to make it easier for entrepreneurs to understand and comply with their rules and requirements.

GLOSSARY

Overhead Costs: These are costs that you have to pay just to be in your business – even if you make no sales. They include rent, rates, electricity, staff etc. Think of them as what you have to pay just to keep a roof 'overhead'.

Cost of Goods Sold: These are costs that you only have to pay because you sell something to someone. So, put simply, if you sell them a sandwich, you have part of the cost of a loaf of bread, the cost of some slices of ham and the cost of some mustard. Added up these are the Cost of Goods Sold for that sandwich.

Mark-Up: A charge that you add to the cost of something in order to give you a profit. So if you buy a software package for £200 and mark it up by 50 per cent, you'll sell it to your client for £300.

17 Week Seventeen:
Planning for Problems

This week you'll identify possible challenges and risks you'll face in carrying out your plans and work out how you would tackle these challenges.

Congratulations, you've now completed the most difficult part of putting your business plan together. Soon we'll draw together all your research and planning into a financial projection, but first you need to 'stress test' your business plan.

Any bank manager or investor will want you to have thought about what problems you could face, what could go wrong, and how you might deal with those situations. Nobody, repeat nobody, who is experienced in business will expect (or even think for a moment) that your business will turn out exactly as predicted in your business plan. So they'll want to see that you're prepared for a wide range of possibilities, as they know this kind of adaptability is the key to success.

Challenges

What could cause a challenge to your business? The potential challenges could come from the following directions:

- **Political**. Laws could change, public funding can be changed or removed, and regulations can be changed.

- **Economic**. Interest rates can make debt more expensive. Currency exchange rates can fluctuate and affect the cost of your raw materials or your competitiveness in a foreign market. A recession could put your customers or suppliers out of business, or mean that your products or services are further down the list of priorities for your customers.

- **Social**. Your kind of services could go out of fashion, someone else's brand could become more fashionable, people might be retiring earlier, or working until later in life, more people might start living in city centres rather than suburbs, there might be a new 'craze' for a particular type of children's toy, a trend to shorter working hours, or any of a whole variety of social changes.

- **Technological**. A new technology could be invented that makes your services less useful or valuable; a technological breakthrough could mean that your customers need your product to develop too.

- **Environmental**. What will changes in climate do to your business? What about a really wet summer? A warm winter? Could environmental pressure groups start campaigning on an issue that affects your business?

- **Competitive**. What could your competitors do to create challenges for you? Drop prices? Release a newer, better product? Offer a better service? Run a big advertising campaign? Target your customers with special offers?

This is known as the PESTEC framework by consultants, but they use Cultural as the 'C'. I (and quite a few others) believe cultural challenges are covered under the Social heading, and that Competitive challenges are an important consideration to take into account. Your bank manager or investors will have heard of the PESTEC framework (and will be pleased to see that you have too), so be prepared to answer a question about why you are using Competitive rather than Cultural. Also, they may have learned about it many years ago when it was only known as the PEST framework, so be prepared to explain the two new sections.

Trends

From all your research into your industry and your marketplace, you should have a good feeling for what the trends are. This will include knowledge such as:

- Is the demand for your kind of products or services growing or shrinking?
- What's happening to the pricing?
- What's happening to the cost of raw materials?
- Are there new companies entering the marketplace all the time?
- Is anyone going out of business? Why?

There will be other important trends in your industry and your marketplace. You need to identify them. So, for example, in the ice cream industry in the UK one trend is for developing ice creams based on well-known chocolate and confectionery brands and, at the upper end of the market, there is also a trend for specialist-branded higher-value, higher-quality ice cream in smaller round tubs.

Risks

There are also many risks within your plans. For example, a supplier might suddenly increase prices or you might sell less than you were expecting:

- What are the assumptions in your plan that could turn out to be wrong?
- Where could things change?
- What does the worst case scenario look like?

Identify and list the risks within your business that could affect your plans.

Planning for these challenges, trends and risks

Spend this week looking at all the possible things that could cause you a problem in your business. Then select the most likely, and also the most serious, and develop an action plan of what you would do to save the day if each situation happened. Write this up into a two-page report for your business plan, listing the potential challenges under the PESTEC headings.

Next, write a short summary of the current trends you actually see in your industry and your marketplace, what these could mean for your business, and what these indicate about the likelihood of the challenges you identified above.

Next, write a section on risks within your plans.

Finally, write about how you will mitigate or manage these challenges, trends and risks. Do you need to take out insurance? Do you need to take specialist training? Do you need to hire an expert in a particular field? Do you need to have a Plan B for something that could be risky?

And what about the effects of these problems? What kind of a drop in sales could they lead to? What kind of a rise in costs could they bring? We'll use these figures to test your financial projections later.

Don't panic!

It may be quite worrying to see this list of terrible things that could happen. We're deliberately looking at all the worst things that could happen in your business. If you applied the same thought process to living in your house or working for your current employer, you could come up with lots of really scary things that could happen too. That doesn't mean they'll happen!

Insurance

One of the ways of planning for risk is to have insurance. Some insurance is legally required – so if you have employees you must have Employer's Liability Insurance, or if you sell direct to the public you might have to have Public Liability Insurance.

Other insurance is optional but often worth having – such as Buildings and Contents Insurance for your premises and the things inside it, to cover you against, fire, flood, burglary and so on. If you're some kind of specialist consultant you may need Professional Indemnity Insurance to cover you in the event of giving bad advice to a client that leads to problems for them. Some clients insist on you having that insurance before they'll buy from you.

Most big insurance companies do 'bundles' of cover so you can get the most common types of insurance for businesses rolled into one package.

Other insurance often isn't worth it, such as extended warranties on electrical goods – you end up paying almost as much as the replacement cost of the item anyway for a very slim chance that it might get lost or damaged. Seek advice from your accountant and mentor about which insurances are worth having.

Emma and Alan

It turns out that Alan is very good at identifying potential problems and he creates a big list of outside threats, risks within their plans and trends that will affect their business.

At first Emma is quite deflated by this and spends a day feeling a bit down – perhaps their plans can't work after all! Perhaps she'd better stick to the day job.

But then her mentor reminds her that these are all the worst things that could happen. It doesn't mean they will. By identifying them now, they can plan to avoid them as best as possible, and he's really impressed that they've taken the time to even think about these potential risks as it'll make them much more likely to succeed.

Her spirits lifted a bit, Emma meets Alan for a drink and they work out how they can minimise all these potential risks.

Opportunities

This approach can also be used to work through positive opportunities that might arise, and it can be a good antidote to the activities of this week to do the exercise in this way.

Shared Experiences

Bill Gates is the founder of Microsoft. He believes it's vitally important to be on the lookout for new ideas, new trends and new challenges:

'You have to have your feelers out at all times, for example, in the technical field having great relations with universities to see what they're doing, what they're thinking about, but also reaching out to the leading people and getting them to critique your strategy, making sure that you're not being insular about those things. It's very important because something that's small now can turn into something very large over a period of years and if you wait until it gets large before you say, oh, okay we should do that too, then you're probably too late to adapt your strategy in that direction. We have so many examples of companies like Wang that did the word processor, was very successful and then that was it. They didn't, you know, go on to the next thing.'

THIS WEEK'S TO DO LIST

- [ ] Work through the PESTEC framework and think of all the things that could happen that would challenge your plans.

- [ ] Go through the list you have made and work out what you would do in each situation to make the most of it and keep your business on track.

- [ ] List the current trends in your industry and marketplace as identified from your research.

- [ ] Identify possible risk areas in your plans.

- [ ] Work out how to manage all these risks.

- [ ] Write up this section of your business plan.

18 Week Eighteen: Profit Forecast

> This week you'll set your prices, forecast your sales and, most importantly of all, you'll work out if you can make a profit.

You've now nearly finished your business plan. All that remains is to take your ideas and plans and put some numbers to them!

But before we can get down to the details of your financial plans, you need to make a few key decisions...

Setting your prices

The two biggest challenges in putting together your forecast will be estimating how many sales you will make and deciding what price you will sell at.

There is no scientific, straightforward answer to the question of 'What price should I charge?' It's an art form, balancing many different considerations:

- What is the highest price you can get from your customers?

- What is your business model? Cheap and cheerful? Or luxury, love and large price tags?

- What does it cost you to provide your customers with the product or service? Your price will need to be more than this – preferably lots more!

- What do your competitors charge? And do you want to be perceived as being cheaper than them or better than them?

- Are the prices already set by your suppliers? This may be particularly true for retailers, where the prices are marked on the products by the manufacturer and that is what the customer expects to pay.

Remember that you'll be doing your customers no favours by setting your prices too low and going out of business in six months' time. Set a price that earns you a good profit.

You may need to experiment with your pricing during your first year until you get it right, but remember that it's much harder to raise your prices than it is to lower them – better to start at the high end and do special offers to test ideal price points.

Emma

Emma and Alan research the prices at other sandwich shops and cafés in the area, and they also work out the costs in terms of ingredients, time to prepare and contribution to their overheads.

They decide that Racing Greens is in the luxury end of the market and should be priced accordingly. They also decide that it fits with their branding to have a really simple, clear pricing system so they should price in round numbers rather than prices ending in 99p. They set their prices at £4 for a regular salad, £6 for a large, with luxury salads being £2 more. They decide on £2.50 for a fresh juice drink and £3 for a soup. They also have an option to design your own salad starting at £4 for the base salad and 50p per topping.

They will make this seem good value in their customers' eyes by only using the freshest, healthiest ingredients and by making the portions generous.

Forecasting your sales

Before you get on to more detailed financial forecasts, you need to work out how much you can sell in each month in your first year.

To do this, start a spreadsheet or a piece of paper with the columns for each of the first 12 months of your business and then add the following rows:

1. Product 1 Price

2. Product 1 Unit Sales

3. PRODUCT 1 SALES VALUE

4. Product 2 Price

5. Product 2 Unit Sales

6. PRODUCT 2 SALES VALUE

And so on. You can do the same with services or billable hours. Replace product numbers with product names. Put the price in all the columns. Now for the forecasting. In the Unit Sales row, put in each month the number of units or hours that you think you can sell of that product or service.

You can estimate the number of units you will sell in a month by starting with thinking about how many you could sell in a day.

Emma

Emma and Alan do this by spending their lunch hours for a week standing outside different sandwich shops in the area and counting the number of customers who buy from there in a two-hour period. Emma does the first hour, then Alan takes his lunch break an hour later to take over.

They then see the pattern of when people shop for lunch and get an average figure of how many people buy from a shop during the lunch period. This figure is 172. They decide that it's realistic to assume that it will take them nearly a year to reach this average number of customers per day, and they guesstimate that they will have 20 per cent of the average in month 1, 30 per cent of the average in month 2, and so on, until month 9 when they have the same average number of customers as other local sandwich shops.

So they estimate that they'll have 688 sales in their first month. They then allocate these between the different products, taking account of the fact that people will normally buy a drink with their salad, most people will buy a regular salad and a fairly small proportion will buy the largest luxury meals.

A business selling salads would normally be quite seasonal, but Emma and Alan plan to sell hot salads in winter (such as honey-roasted carrots with feta and nuts), so they don't forecast a drop in sales then. They do forecast lower sales in August, however, when many of the office workers will be on holiday, and in December and January, which are effectively only three-week months because of the holidays.

The difficulty with forecasting

Forecasting your financial incomings and outgoings at this stage in your business is incredibly difficult and some of the numbers are, frankly, going to be guesses. That's OK, but you have to have some reasoning to back up these guesses.

Remember that in this book I'm assuming your business is fairly simple and straightforward, and that you are starting on a small scale. If this is not the case, then you need to supplement the advice in this book with the advice in *The Definitive Business Plan* by Richard Stutely. I've used his book to help me write plans for my businesses and have found it immensely helpful. (see Week Twenty's 'Recommended Reading' on p.159.)

The Profit Forecast

The first place to start is with what bankers, accountants and investors call a Profit and Loss Forecast – but, being entrepreneurs, we'll be positive and focus on what we want to achieve and call it a Profit Forecast. This shows what sales you expect to make and at what price, what the cost of these sales will be (raw materials etc.) and what your overheads will be (what you need to pay just to keep the roof over your head). Once you subtract the costs from the sales, you'll have your profit.

It's easiest to do this on a computer spreadsheet. Initially, do the forecast for 12 months, with one column for each month's forecast figures. We're going to assume at this point that you won't register for VAT, though this may change later.

You should put each figure in at the point that the sale is completed – regardless of when the sale is paid for. So if someone phones up and orders 20 of your product on 1 February, but they have a credit account with you so they don't have to pay until 1 March, then the sale would be registered in your profit forecast in February – the point at which you invoice them for the sale. Likewise, if you buy from your supplier on 26 February, they send you the invoice (the bill) dated 2 March but you don't have to pay until 2 April, the purchase would appear as a cost in your Profit Forecast for March.

Start with your sales forecasts. Use a separate row for each of your products or services, and then go across the columns putting in your forecast Sales Value for each product as forecast above. Under these rows, do a line for Total Sales and add up each month's sales in this row.

Next, do the section for Cost of Sales. So, if you were starting a company making computers, then for each computer that you are forecasting to sell above, you need to list the cost of the box, the disc drive, the memory, the processor and so on, here. Do a row for each type of purchase you'll have to make. At the bottom of this section put a row for Total Cost of Sales. Make sure that the figures you enter include the VAT that your suppliers will charge you, as you can't reclaim this if you're not VAT-registered.

Now do a line called Contribution. (Bank managers and accountants also refer to this as Gross Profit, but personally I think the terms Net and Gross just confuse people. Even Richard Branson confesses to having difficulty remembering what each means. Also I believe that it's dangerous to refer to it as a profit at this stage, as you still have plenty to pay for!) This is the contribution that your sales make towards your overheads. To calculate it for each month of your forecast, take the month's Total Sales and subtract the month's Total Cost of Sales.

Next, you're on to the Overheads section. Remember, this is everything you need to pay in order to keep a roof over your head – costs you have to pay even if you don't sell anything. The following are ideas of things you may need under this heading: Rent, Rates, Water, Electricity, Other Charges (dustbins etc.), Wages (including yours), Employer's Costs (National Insurance etc. – allow 30 per cent of the amount you put in wages for this), Travel and Entertainment Expenses, Accountants' Fees, Lawyers' Fees, Bank Charges, Stationery, Postage and Couriers, Marketing Materials (leaflets, websites etc.), Insurance, Advertising, Telephones, Leasing Charges, Tax and, of course, no forecast would be complete without a line for 'Miscellaneous'. Again, remember to include VAT in these estimates.

Don't put in any of the high-value equipment, vehicles or other machinery that you need to buy to set up your business. Instead, at the bottom of this section put a line titled 'Depreciation'. In here you should put a value that you calculate as follows: the total value of the equipment you're going to buy, multiplied by 0.25 and then divided by 12. What this calculation does is take a quarter of the cost of the equipment into account each year for four years. The idea is that the only cost to you is the value you are losing on the equipment by keeping it and using it. So depreciation is the cost of ownership.

Add a line below this called Total Overheads, and you can guess what to put in this row!

Below this put a line for Operating Profit (also known as 'the bottom line'). This line should show the Contribution minus the Total Overheads.

The moment of truth

Now that you have a forecast, there are some important calculations to make to see if it works!

Your breakeven point for the year

This is the amount of sales required to make a profit in your business in the 12 months of this forecast. To calculate it:

1. Add up all your monthly Total Sales to get a figure for the year. Call this figure A.

2. Add up all your Total Cost of Sales to get a figure for the year. Call this figure B.

3. Add up all your Total Overheads to get a figure for the year. Call this figure C.

4. The first calculation is A minus B to get the total Contribution (Gross Profit) for the year. Call this figure D.

5. Next, calculate this as a percentage of sales: D divided by A, then multiplied by 100. Call this figure E.

6. Finally, calculate your breakeven point: C divided by E, then multiplied by 100.

The result is the amount of sales you need to make in order to make a profit – your breakeven point.

Do your total sales pass the breakeven point during the year? If not, how far away from your breakeven point are you over the year (i.e. how does the breakeven point compare with your Total Sales (figure A) for the whole year? Is there a way you could realistically:

- Increase your sales over the year?

- Reduce your cost of sales over the year?

- Reduce your overheads over the year?

You can also continue forecasting further into the future until you can show six months of continued profitability at the end of your forecast.

Is it ever going to be possible to pass your breakeven point? If not, it's time to think seriously about your business model. You're either not selling enough, not charging enough, or your costs are too high. If you can't fix these, you may have to look at another idea. Time for a conversation with your mentor!

If it's going to take a long time (more than twelve months) for your sales to reach breakeven, that may also indicate a problem in your forecast. Talk to your mentor or accountant. This may be OK if yours is a very new type of product or service and it's going to take a while to test, educate and grow the market – but you'll need to have funding for your business in the meantime and we'll look at that next week.

Your monthly breakeven point

If you do reach breakeven in your first six months or so and you're happy with your forecast, then you can continue by calculating your monthly breakeven point.

This is simply the breakeven point you calculated above, divided by 12. This tells you how much you must sell *every* month to break even.

This is an important figure for you to manage your business with, and your bank manager will want to see that you have done this calculation.

THIS WEEK'S TO DO LIST

- ☐ Decide if you'll register for VAT (see Week Twenty-One for more information on VAT).

- ☐ Decide on prices for your products or services.

- ☐ Forecast your sales.

- ☐ Forecast your profit.

- ☐ Calculate your breakeven point and assess your plan against this.

- ☐ Start to think about your company structure (more about this in Week Twenty-One).

THIS WEEK'S RECOMMENDED READING

Accounts Demystified, by Anthony Rice (Pearson).

The clearest guide to understanding business forecasting and accounts there is – great if you don't really like dealing with numbers. This book will come in particularly handy when you start to grow and have to produce more detailed financial reports.

19 Week Nineteen:
Cash Flow Forecast

This week you'll plan how the money will flow in and out of your business and decide if you're going to need any finance to start the business.

You now know when you'll be able to make your business profitable, and how much profit you can make. Profitability is good, but the most important part of planning and running your business is forecasting and managing the flow of cash in and out of the business.

Think of it like food. You sit down and work out what food you're going to be supplied with in the next year and calculate that you're going to get more food than you could possibly eat during that time. You'll even have some to store away for next year. Unfortunately, what your estimate for the year doesn't show is that you only get one small packet of crisps each month for the next 11 months, then in month 12 a huge lorry is going to roll up outside your house to deliver the rest. Would you still be alive to be able to enjoy that feast?

Your business is the same, except it feeds on money. If it runs out of money for a while, then it becomes very, very sick, and can even die. It doesn't matter that it will get a huge feast of cash in a few months. Running out of cash and watching your business suffer is a horrible thing to go through, but many entrepreneurs experience it. Often that experience is enough to spur them on to make it work and ensure they never have to go through that again.

You need to plan the flow of cash so that your business always has enough to eat, and hopefully you can avoid this experience.

The Cash Flow Forecast

You set this out in very much the same way as a Profit Forecast but, instead of showing when the sale is made, you put in the amounts when the bill is paid. So a cash payment is shown in exactly the same place, but a payment on invoice will be shown in the next month.

You have a section at the top for Income, then you add up Total Income at the bottom of this section.

Next, you have a section for Expenditure. This includes all the supplier costs and other costs that go to make up your cost of sales, as well as your overhead costs. Remember that suppliers will mostly also charge you VAT.

You should also include in here, on a row called Capital Expenditure, the full cost of any equipment, vehicles or other machinery that you will need to buy to run your business, and you should include them at the full cost you will buy them for and when you will have to pay for them. Don't also include the row titled Depreciation that you have in your Profit Forecast as they are for the same items.

At the bottom of this, you add up all the values to give Total Expenditure.

Then you have a line called Opening Balance, a line below this called Cash Inflow (Outflow) and a line below that called Closing Balance.

In month 1 the Opening Balance is zero. Then the Cash Inflow (Outflow) is Total Income minus Total Expenditure. The Closing Balance is the Opening Balance plus the Cash Inflow (Outflow).

In all the other months, the Opening Balance is the Closing Balance from the month before. The other two calculations are the same.

How does it look?

If you don't have any negative figures at all, even in the early months, then your business is a miracle – go and check the figures again. Perhaps get your mentor to take a look, or your accountant (when you get one – see Week Twenty-One). If your figures are correct, then congratulations – you seem to have a cracking good business!

If you have some negative figures in the first half of your business plan, that's to be expected. The key is, what is the largest negative figure? This is how much finance you need to get into the business. Does it make your eyes water? If so, get some advice from your accountant or mentor.

If there are mostly negative figures throughout your cash flow, then there's a problem with your business model and you need to revisit the number of sales you plan to make, what costs you have and other factors. Your accountant and mentor can advise you. Again, though, the exception to this is if you're working long term to build quite a large business, or a product or service that is new and different and will take time to establish a market. You just have to be sure you can get the funding.

Funding your business

In order to be able to feed your business with the money it needs to live, you need to raise funding for at least the largest negative number on your cash flow forecast. It's actually much wiser to raise a fair bit more than this to be prepared for unexpected events.

I go into much more detail on this complex subject in my book *How to Fund Your Business*, but here I'll give a brief overview.

Funding can come from one, or more, of the following sources:

Your customers. This is nearly always overlooked – but it's absolutely the best way to fund a start-up! Your customers want your service, so can you use your entrepreneurial charm to persuade them to pay you for it in advance?

You. Do you and your business partners have savings that you could invest in the company?

Friends and family. Would any of your friends or family invest in your business, or give you a cheap or interest-free loan?

Asset finance. If your business involves using expensive equipment, vehicles or other high-value assets, then it's often better to lease these. Sometimes this can be arranged through the supplier, otherwise banks and specialist finance companies can provide this kind of finance. It can be leasing, hire purchase or other similar schemes. It means you can pay for your equipment over a longer period of time in small payments, rather than buying it outright at the start of your business. In a B2B company, one asset is the invoices you have sent out but not yet been paid for – you can get a 'factoring' or 'invoice discounting' finance company to pay you up to 85 per cent of the value of these on the day you invoice, then they collect the money when it becomes due and pay you the rest minus their finance fee. This is quite expensive finance but it can take a lot of the worry away regarding chasing debts. Get advice from your accountant on all these schemes.

Bank overdraft. This is one of the first sources of finance that most entrepreneurs look to, but not necessarily the best. It can be suitable if you are just expecting to dip in and out of it to fund brief periods of cash shortage for relatively short amounts, but if you plan to be permanently overdrawn for six months it's an expensive way to borrow.

Bank loan. This is another of the first options selected by many start-ups, but beware of saddling your business with debt from the start. Is there any way of raising the money as investments from you, friends, family or angel investors (see the next page)? If you really prefer debt finance to equity (investment) finance, then that's up to you of course, but you may find it difficult to start with. The bank may want personal guarantees or other security in the form of property (your house) or a guarantee from another family member. This is very risky and I advise against it, but you should seek professional advice. If you're not able to provide security, you may be able to get a loan guarantee from the government. This used to be called the Small Firms Loan Guarantee scheme, but it's now called the Enterprise Finance Guarantee scheme. Under this scheme the government gives the bank a guarantee that they will pay up to 75 per cent of the loan if you go out of business, and in return you pay a fee to the government. You can find out more details at **www.bis.gov.uk/efg**.

Soft loan. A soft loan is one with little or no interest charged on it. If you're not able to get enough funding from the sources above and you're under 30, then you may be eligible for a soft loan from the Prince's Trust. There are some other soft loan schemes too, and you can find details of these on the websites listed in the 'List of Contacts' on pp.154–55.

Grant. Again, the Prince's Trust offers grants to young people starting in business, but there are a host of other grants available too. See the websites recommended below for details. In general, grants don't allow you to have started what it is you need the grant for before you're given the grant – so check all the rules before getting too advanced in opening your business. The point of the grant is that it helps you do something that you wouldn't otherwise have been able to afford, and it doesn't look that way if you've already done whatever it is!

Angel investor. These are well-off individuals who have decided to make a proportion of their investments in start-up or early-stage businesses. They do this because, although the risks are high, the rewards can be very high too. Some of them also do it because of a personal interest in the kind of business they invest in or a passion for small business in general. In return for investing money in your company, they will want shares (how many is a matter for negotiation) and some may want to become a director of your company – therefore the most important considerations are: do you like them, do you trust them and could you work with them? Your accountant and mentor can advise you on this, and may be able to put you in touch with local business angels. Some of the networks are given in the 'List of Contacts' below and your Business Link will also be able to put you in touch with some. You may also be able to attract angels by registering under the Enterprise Investment Scheme (EIS). This is a simple scheme run by HMRC to encourage wealthy individuals to invest in early-stage businesses, and it allows your investors to reduce their level of risk and reduce their tax bill – always likely to raise their interest.

Work out a mix of funding that could provide you with the money you require, research suitable sources of such funding and, if necessary, get quotes.

In general, banks will only provide funding that matches funding from other sources, so if you invest £1,000 they'll lend you £1,000. Therefore, you're likely to need other investment, or asset finance, if you want to get any kind of bank funding. Most bank managers will take into account money that you are putting in 'in kind', so if you'll be taking only a small salary from the business they'll count the difference between that and what would be a reasonable salary.

The other thing to note about bank funding is that they don't lend you umbrellas when it's raining! You need to arrange the bank finance now, even if your plan shows you won't need it for six months. If you wait until month 5 or 6, they'll get very jittery about the hole you look like you're going to fall into if they don't give you the money. They'll also have forgotten about all the money you put in at the start and will want new 'matching' money. Sort all the finance out that you need to get to profitability at the start.

Back to your forecasts

Now put these figures back into your forecasts to see if your business works with this funding.

If you'll be using asset finance, you can take out those assets from Capital Expenditure in your Cash Flow Forecast and the associated Depreciation from your Profit Forecast. Instead, just put a line for Asset Finance Charges in the Overheads section of your Profit Forecast and in the Expenditure section of your Cash Flow Forecast, and include the amounts quoted by the finance company.

If you'll be using debt finance (loan, overdraft or soft loan), put two lines in your Profit Forecast under the Operating Profit line. The first line, should read 'Interest Payments' and the second should read 'Profit before Tax'. On the first line, forecast the interest charges based on the terms of the loans available. The Profit before Tax line can be calculated by subtracting Interest Payments from Operating Profit.

If you'll be taking out a loan, in the Cash Flow Forecast insert four lines under the subheading Financing Cash Flow. These lines should go below the Expenditure section of your cash flow, but above the line that says Opening Balance. The first of these new lines should read Loan Money Received, the second line should read Loan Repayments and the third line should read Interest Payments. The fourth line should be Total Financing Cash Inflow (Outflow), and you should then include this total in the line that already exists titled Total Cash Inflow (Outflow) further down.

If you'll be using an overdraft, in the Cash Flow Forecast you should put a line right at the bottom titled Available Overdraft Facility and simply put in the overdraft facility you want to request all the way along this row, allowing readers of your plan to compare the figure for Closing Balance with the facility you plan to have available.

If you'll be raising equity finance, you don't change anything in your Profit Forecast, but you add a section near the bottom of your Cash Flow Forecast titled Financing Cash Flow (if you haven't done this already to show your debt finance). Put a line in this section titled Equity Investment and put in the amount of money you'll raise in investment during the month that you plan to receive it. Then have a line for Total Financing Cash Inflow (Outflow) if you haven't done so already and include this total in the line that already exists titled Total Cash Inflow (Outflow) further down.

If you expect to receive a grant, then include this in the same way as equity finance, but using the line heading Grant Received. You may be able to include some or all of this grant in your Profit Forecast, but your accountant will advise you on that.

You have now completed your Profit Forecast and your Cash Flow Forecast for a properly funded business. Congratulations! Now, go and have a nice drink as a reward for your hard work.

Emma

Emma and Alan calculated that they needed £20,000 of funding to get their shop up and running and fund their business in its first year, allowing some spare for unexpected events.

They decide to lease their display chillers, refrigerators, cooker and other equipment, which they work out reduces their need for other start-up finance by £5,000. Alan has been very careful with his money and has built up substantial savings, but Emma has none. Emma asks her family to give her (personally) an interest-free loan of £2,500, which she will pay back at £50 a month over the next four years. She and Alan then agree that they should invest the same amount in the business. That contributes another £5,000 of funding.

Their accountant suggests that the bank manager may be willing to regard the leasing as contributing £5,000 of investment on top of Emma and Alan's total of £5,000 of investment, and then match this with a £10,000 loan. This is because of the strength of their idea, the fact they have a good mentor and the dedication they obviously have. It's also because they've been prepared to personally invest a sum of money that's significant to each of them. Neither Emma nor Alan own their home or have any other security to offer the bank, so their accountant recommends that they apply under the Enterprise Finance Guarantee scheme.

Shared Experiences

Liz Jackson set up Great Guns Marketing, a telephone marketing agency which has grown very rapidly:

'The bank wouldn't lend me any money so I went to the Prince's Youth Trust and did a business plan for those guys and they gave me a grant for £1,000 and a loan of £4,000 – so that gave me some money to actually buy some second-hand furniture, second-hand fax machine, second-hand computer, phone etc. One of the biggest challenges was actually getting the money and then being able to convince people that I could do something.'

Cliff Stanford set up an internet service provider:

'Around about 1991, on a bulletin board, a number of people made the comment that we'd never get low cost access in the UK. However, I made the comment that if 200 of us got together and put something together

▶

for internet access then it could be done at a cost per head of about £10 per month. Well, a lot of people were keen but I said that I'd need £20,000 to set the company up, and I would need to know I had customers. So, about 150 people sent me cheques for £120, and they didn't know who I was other than what I'd said on this bulletin board! So there was a market there.'

Cliff then had the funding to start Demon Internet, which he later sold his personal stake in for around £30m.

THIS WEEK'S TO DO LIST

- ☐ Prepare your Cash Flow Forecast.
- ☐ Identify the funding you'll require.
- ☐ Decide on the best sources for this funding.
- ☐ Research how to obtain that funding and get quotes if necessary.
- ☐ Include this financing in your forecasts.

THIS WEEK'S RECOMMENDED READING

How to Fund Your Business, by Steve Parks (Pearson).

LIST OF CONTACTS

www.bestmatch.co.uk

The website for the National Business Angels Network.

www.eisa.org.uk

Includes a useful summary of the Enterprise Investment Scheme.

www.grantfinder.co.uk

A website to help you find grants and soft loans.

www.j4b.co.uk

Another website to help you find grants.

www.princes-trust.org.uk

The Prince's Trust – a great organisation to help young people start in business.

www.venturesite.co.uk

Another website for business angels.

20 Week Twenty:
The Business Plan

This week you'll pull together everything you've written in the last few months to form your business plan.

You've done everything you need to do for your business plan. The job this week is to pull all of that together into one document. You can arrange each section as you feel is best to tell a story of your business that flows well, but I'd suggest:

1. Company Vision and Values (written in Week Twelve)

2. Founders (written in Week Five)

3. The Opportunity (written in Week Nine)

4. Customers (written in Week Ten)

5. Competitors (written in Week Eleven)

6. Sales (written in Week Thirteen)

7. Resources (written in Week Fifteen)

8. Suppliers (written in Week Sixteen)

9. Challenges, Threats and Risks (written in Week Seventeen)

10. Profit Forecast (written in Week Eighteen)

11. Cash Flow Forecast (written in Week Nineteen)

Reviewing the plan

You're very likely to find that there are whole sections you want to rewrite as a result of what you've learned in later weeks, so don't be dismayed if that's the case. I've kept this week brief to allow you plenty of time to rewrite it quite substantially!

Make sure that your plan flows, is easy to read, is well presented – simple and clear rather than flashy – and that it makes sense. Read it through from beginning to end and ask yourself these questions, pretending that you're a bank manager who knows nothing about the business except what's in this plan:

- Do I understand what this business will do?

- Is it clear why this business will do it better than anyone else?

- Is it clear that people want to pay for what this business does?

- Do I understand how the business will find and sell to customers?

- Do the management understand the industry and the marketplace?

- Do the management appreciate the challenges ahead and have they prepared for them?

- How much finance is going to be needed and where will it come from?

- Is the business financially viable and can it make good profits?

- Can the business survive on the cash it will have available?

You'll probably want to do some more work on the plan after this exercise in order to be certain that all these questions are clearly answered.

Executive Summary

Once you're happy with the main plan, you need to write what is called an Executive Summary. This is a one-page (it can be two, but try and make it one if possible) summary of the whole plan.

In this summary you should have one paragraph that summarises each section of your plan.

At the bottom you should give these key financial details:

- The business will break even once annual sales of £(amount) are reached. The management expect the business to break even in (month)(year).

- The Turnover (Total Sales) in the first year will be £(amount).

- The Profit/Loss in the first year will be £(amount).

- The business will raise initial funding of £(amount) through equity investment by the management/external equity investment/bank loan/other loan/grant (just show the ones that apply).

- The business will apply for an overdraft facility of £(amount) (only if required). The peak borrowing will be £(maximum amount you expect to go into overdraft from your cash flow forecast) and will occur in (month).

If you're planning to raise money through selling equity (shares), then say how many shares you plan to issue and at what price per share.

Test your plans on others

Now you have a business plan that is ready for the outside world. Before you take it to the outside world, send it to your mentor and a few friends or colleagues whom you trust and respect. Let them read it over the next week, and ask for their reactions and feedback by the end of the week.

Book meetings with banks and professional advisers

Over the last couple of months you've been collecting recommendations for bank managers, accountants and lawyers. Set up appointments to meet a selection of each next week. You should also send your plan to them, so that they can give you feedback when you meet.

Shared Experiences

Trenton Moss, founder of Webcredible:

'I didn't need to raise any funding to get the business off the ground, but I still did a business plan because everyone advised me that I would find it a useful document just for myself to help me steer the business and stay focused. I'd advise anyone else to do the same.'

THIS WEEK'S TO DO LIST

☐ Assemble your business plan from your work over the last few months.

☐ Read through your plan.

☐ Rewrite parts of it.

☐ Check your plan again.

☐ Rewrite parts of it.

☐ Write an Executive Summary.

☐ Get others to check your plan.

☐ Rewrite parts of it.

☐ Check your plan again.

(I'm not kidding about all the checking and rewriting!)

THIS WEEK'S RECOMMENDED READING

The Definitive Business Plan, by Richard Stutely (Pearson).

This book will be useful if you're planning to start a larger business and need a more advanced business plan than we cover here – perhaps if you decide you need substantial external funding.

21 Week Twenty-One:
Banks and Advisers

This week you'll meet with the professional advisers and bank managers who hope you'll choose them to guide you through running your business.

Meeting the bank managers

The aim of the meeting is for you to outline your idea to the bank manager and for the bank manager to outline to you how they can help. This is your chance to see if you can work with them. It's just a first meeting and you don't need to sign up to anything.

Throughout the meeting, ask yourself:

- Do I like this person?

- Do I trust them?

- Will they be willing to help me out as much as possible if things don't go as planned or are they a jobsworth?

- Are their comments and suggestions helpful and constructive?

- Does this person actually have any authority within the bank?

Ask the bank manager:

- Are you the person I'll be dealing with day to day? If they're not, ask to meet the person who will be.

- What's your package offer for start-ups?

- What's your experience of helping start-ups?

- Can you give an example of how you've helped another start-up business overcome a particular unexpected challenge in the past?

- What lending authority do you personally have without referring to anyone else?

This last point is important because some of the high street banks have gone down the route of removing any actual power from the business account managers. They have become 'relationship' managers, and their job is to meet you and then write a report for a central office somewhere else where they actually make the decisions – you're then not allowed to speak to anyone in this central office to make your case, so you have to rely on the 'Chinese whispers' being accurate, and rely on the bank manager to communicate your ideas and needs positively. In my experience this just doesn't work.

Inside the bank manager's mind

In the first meeting, they'll focus almost exclusively on you as a person. So what will they be looking for?

- **Enthusiasm**. They'll want to know that you really want to do this and that you believe that you can.

- **Tenacity**. They'll need to believe that you have the get-up-and-go to see through what will be a difficult job.

- **Research**. They'll want to see that you've put the time into working out your idea, your market, who your customers will be and why they will buy.

- **Realism**. They don't expect you to become a millionaire in year one with no problems – and they don't expect you to believe that either. They'll want to see that you're prepared for the challenges ahead and willing to operate within your financial means rather than going straight out to buy the company Jaguar. They'll want to see that you've thought of some of the things that could go wrong.

- **Adaptability**. If you know there'll be problems and challenges, and they do, they'll want to see that you can adapt your business to cope with these. What will your Plan B be?

Sadly, these days the key thing at the front of their mind is which banking products they can sell to you so that they make their targets for that month. So they'll try to sell you insurance, invoice finance and much more. Be aware that it's for their benefit that they are offering you these products and if you decide you actually need them you'll be able to get much better value equivalents from other providers.

Questions they're likely to ask you

- Why do you want to start a business?

- Why will you be successful?

- What do you know about this market and the line of business?

- How will you find your first customers?

If you want bank finance

If your business plan shows that you will want to raise finance from the bank, then the bank manager is going to be measuring up you and your idea under a seven-point checklist known by the acronym 'PARSERS', which starts with the most important considerations to them and works down the priorities:

- **Person**. Do they think you have what it takes? Do they like you? Are you professional? Do you know what you're talking about? Have you got the background experience? Have you got the persistence and confidence that it will take?

- **Amount**. How much you will be looking to borrow, and what for. This won't really be covered until a later meeting, but they'll have a rough estimate in their head.

- **Repayment**. If you're going to borrow money, will you be able to repay it? They'll be weighing up your financial resources.

- **Security**. If you're looking to borrow money, what security will they be able to fall back on if you don't end up being able to repay?

- **Expediency**. How quickly will you be able to repay?

- **Remuneration**. How much money could the bank earn from providing you with finance?

- **Services**. What other products can the bank provide you with to earn money – credit cards, asset finance, insurance, pensions etc.?

So prepare for the meeting in advance and be sure you can guide the manager through the key points in your business plan that will allow them to tick these items on their checklist.

If the bank manager isn't keen to lend you the money you want to borrow because you don't have enough security, then ask them about the Enterprise Finance Guarantee scheme from the government.

After the meetings

Note down your thoughts on each manager's strengths and weaknesses.

From now on, keep in touch with the bank managers you felt you could work with and don't bother keeping in touch with those you felt you couldn't.

Start negotiating with these managers on the packages they can offer you and the financing they can provide, if you need that.

Deciding on a bank manager – the decision grid

When making any key decision about your business, it's best to use a 'decision grid' to help you balance out all the factors.

A decision grid is where you write down the names of the things or people you're trying to decide between along the top of a column each, then down the left-hand side you list the things that are important to you in making the decision.

You also include a column for 'weighting'. This is the score you give to each factor in the decision, based on how important you think that factor is. Use a number between 1 and 10.

You then give each thing a score under each factor and multiply that score by the weighting.

So, let's say you're using a decision grid to choose cheese to serve at a dinner party (I don't suggest you really do this, people will think you've really lost it. This is just an easy example.)

You're trying to choose between brie, stilton and cheddar. You decide that the important factors in your decision are how posh the cheese is seen to be (it's a dinner party after all), how ready the cheese in the supermarket is to eat, what price the cheese is and how much you like the cheese yourself.

So a decision grid based on this would look like:

Factor	Weighting	Brie	Stilton	Cheddar
Poshness				
Ready to Eat				
Price				
Like				

You now need to give a weighting to each factor based on how important it will be in your decision. Use numbers between 1 and 10 – the higher the number, the more important the factor.

Factor	Weighting	Brie	Stilton	Cheddar
Poshness	7			
Ready to Eat	8			
Price	4			
Like	6			

So in this case, it's more important that the cheese will be nice and ready to eat, and less important what it costs. You rate whether your friends will think it's posh higher than whether you actually like it... You're so middle class.

The next step is to give each cheese a score under each factor and to multiply this score by the weighting to get the final score.

Factor	Weighting	Brie	Stilton	Cheddar
Poshness	7	8 x 7 = 56	7 x 7 = 49	2 x 7 = 14
Ready to Eat	8	3 x 8 = 24	7 x 8 = 56	9 x 8 = 72
Price	4	2 x 4 = 8	2 x 4 = 8	7 x 4 = 28
Like	6	8 x 6 = 48	5 x 6 = 30	2 x 6 = 12

So:

- The brie is posh, not ready to eat, expensive, but you really like it.

- The stilton is fairly posh, reasonably ready to eat, expensive, and you don't mind it.

- The cheddar isn't very posh, ready to eat, fairly cheap, but you don't like it much.

You now have weighted scores for each cheese under each factor in the decision. The next thing is to add them up.

Factor	Weighting	Brie	Stilton	Cheddar
Poshness	7	8 x 7 = 56	7 x 7 = 49	2 x 7 = 14
Ready to Eat	8	3 x 8 = 24	7 x 8 = 56	9 x 8 = 72
Price	4	2 x 4 = 8	2 x 4 = 8	7 x 4 = 28
Like	6	8 x 6 = 48	5 x 6 = 30	2 x 6 = 12
TOTAL		136	143	126

So, the stilton wins.

Decision grids are a great way of making decisions between a number of things, based on a number of different factors. Use them when you next buy a car or a smartphone – they'll be a great help! They'll also be very useful in your business.

Meeting the accountants

These meetings will be very similar to the meetings you had with the bank managers, in that they're about finding out who you can work with. The key difference is that you aren't going to try to borrow money from your accountant – so remember that you're the paying customer and they have to impress you more than you need to impress them.

These are the services you should be looking for from an accountant:

- Helping you set up your company.

- Helping you refine your business plan.

- Helping you find the funding you need.

- Doing your annual accounts from your records in a year's time.

- Dealing with Corporation Tax and other enquiries from HMRC – perhaps even doing your personal tax returns.

Some key things to ask:

- Will they give you a fixed-price quotation for the services you need for your business?

- Will they agree not to do any work outside this without providing you with a quotation first and you agreeing to it?

- When will you have to pay?

- Will it be the person you're meeting who you'll be dealing with?

- Do they have much experience of start-up businesses?

- Can they give you examples of how they've really helped start-up businesses?

- Have they worked with businesses in your industry/marketplace before?

- Will they help you get started on the understanding that you can't pay them until the business is properly started?

- What software packages or web services will they accept you doing your accounts on?

- What feedback do they have on your business plan? (If they just say non-specific nice things, then they're not going to be a very useful accountant – award extra points to any accountant who can demonstrate that they've actually read it, and who really makes you think about key elements of your plan.)

- What are their thoughts on the company legal structure you should adopt? (see the next page)

- What are their thoughts on the funding you're seeking?

If there's going to be quite a lot to keep track of financially, or if you aren't very financially skilled, it may also be worth using a book-keeping service to do your accounts once a week or once a month. This is relatively cheap and can take away a lot of the painful numbers work that so many entrepreneurs hate! See if the accountants you meet can recommend any book-keepers.

Once you've met all the accountants on your shortlist, do a decision grid in the same way you did for the bank managers, but this time use it to decide on one accountant.

A good accountant can be an incredible help to your business, using their experience and contacts to advise and support you on a wide range of things. They can do much more than add up (or, in the case of a start-up business, subtract!).

Meeting the lawyers

Outline your plans for the business, and get their feedback, but specifically you want their advice on :

- The contracts for any premises you might need.

- The contracts for any equipment you might be leasing.

- The terms for any funding you may need.

- The best company structure (see the next page).

If you're going to be hiring staff soon, you also need to discuss this with the lawyers as you'll need to put employment contracts in place.

Get quotes from each lawyer setting out the services they think you'll need and their quote for that service. Discuss these with your mentor.

Company structure

There are different ways of structuring your company. You can be a sole trader (if there's just one of you), a partnership (if there are two or more of you) or a limited company (however many of you there are).

Sole trader and partnership are the easiest structures to set up, as you don't actually need to do anything! However, it would be highly advisable to write a partnership agreement in the latter case, which would set out how much money each person is putting in, what happens if anyone wants to take money out, what happens if there's a disagreement and what happens if someone leaves or dies. If you adopt this structure look through books and the web for sample agreements, adapt them and then get a lawyer to look over them.

These two forms of operating are simply you operating as a business: you'd have a separate bank account for your business payments, but the business is legally you. If it has debts, they're yours; if someone wants to take the business to court, they sue you personally; and any income it has is yours and you get taxed on it personally.

The advantage of being a sole trader is simplicity. If there's more than one of you starting this business, I'd recommend you choose a limited company structure, but it's best to get some professional advice. Personally I don't think partnerships have any advantages. They're too messy when there are arguments or when someone wants to move on.

A limited company is a separate legal entity that allows your company to stand on its own. The advantages of this are:

- **Protection**. It's the company, not you personally, that has to deal with its debts, litigation, legal obligations etc. (unless you've managed the company very badly indeed, in which case you can become personally liable). You won't lose your house if it all goes wrong.

- **Professionalism**. Particularly if you are running a B2B or a larger-scale B2C, having a proper limited company makes you seem more established and successful.

With the protection that a limited company gives comes responsibility. You have to file your accounts with Companies House once a year, and file an annual return stating the company's address, directors, share capital and shareholders. You also have to notify Companies House on a one-page form if a new director or company secretary joins, or if an old one leaves. There are a few other occasions when you have to notify them, but in general the paperwork is simple and your accountant will often handle it all for you.

I always prefer to take the limited company structure for any business I start, and that's what I'll assume you'll do in this book. If you don't, however, just ignore those steps. As a sole trader or proprietor you don't need to register your business at all.

Talk over the possible company structures with your mentor and your accountant.

Will you register for VAT?

If you're going to make sales of over £58,000 in the year, then you'll have to register for VAT during the year. In some cases it may be easiest to do this from the very start.

You may also decide to register your business for VAT even if you don't have to. The benefit is that you'll also be able to claim back VAT on things you buy. In the early days of a business, you may have lots of expenditure that includes VAT – for example, new machinery, vehicles, your first batch of stock – but not much income yet. In that instance you'll actually get a cheque back from HMRC. Being VAT-registered also makes your business look bigger and more established, often useful if you are B2B.

But don't rush to a hasty decision based on that. Read through the information you ordered from HMRC in Week Sixteen, talk it over with your accountant and make a decision that way.

In general terms, though, if you're selling to consumers you want to leave registering for VAT until you absolutely have to. If you're selling to business clients it often makes sense to register from the outset of your business. This is because other VAT-registered businesses can claim back VAT so don't mind paying it, but for consumers it bumps up the price of the product dramatically.

Because this book is about helping you get a simple business off the ground to test your idea, I've assumed throughout that, like Emma and Alan, you decide not to register for VAT at this stage.

For help with including VAT in your forecasts, ask your accountant.

Adapt your business plan

Based on the meetings you've had this week, and the feedback from your mentor, colleagues and friends from last week, you may want to make changes to your business plan. This might just be adding in better estimates of the fees for your advisers – but hopefully they've proved their worth by giving you valuable advice on how to improve on your current plans.

They might even point out some big holes in the plan that you hadn't thought of. Don't get down about this, it's perfectly normal. The entrepreneur's reaction is just to think of a creative way to fix the problem.

Once you've got the plan just how you want it, it's time to send it to the potential sources of funding you decided on before, and to ask for meetings with them in Week Twenty-Three.

Emma

Our two young entrepreneurs have received the feedback from their mentors, real and imaginary!

Simon, the father of Emma's boyfriend, says that it's not clear enough how the salads that will be served by Racing Greens will differ from the salads you could get in Marks and Spencer or a local sandwich shop. He suggests they create and include a sample menu – and maybe even make a salad to take to each funding meeting they have to give to the people they're meeting!

Meanwhile, they've been imagining what Anita Roddick would say in response to their plan. They decide that she would suggest that they:

- Have a policy of only sourcing their fruit and vegetables from local suppliers or fair-trade sources.

- Ensure all the fruit and vegetables are organic and GM-free.

- Have a charity that they support with a small donation from each sale going to the charity, and occasional events, competitions etc. There's a local charity that takes inner-city children on short holidays to a country farm to find out about growing food and to have a break in the countryside. They decide to support that charity.

- Use the above items as a marketing tool.

- Approach the local branch of The Body Shop to get them to give out promotional vouchers for Racing Greens with each sale and put some leaflets on the counter.

They build all these ideas into a revised version of their business plan.

Emma and Alan have decided to form a limited company, partly because there are two of them, partly because they've dealing with food and there could be some risk of liability there, and partly because they plan to start a chain of shops and become a big company.

Shared Experiences

Trenton Moss, founder of Webcredible:

'I started Webcredible as a limited company right from the beginning, even though I didn't really need to. The limited liability wasn't much of an issue for me as the business didn't have large overheads or cost of sales, at that stage when it was just me. It was the fact that people at a certain level expect to deal with limited companies, and it seems more professional. It gives you a certain credibility. It also saved me having to convert from being a sole trader to being a limited company at a later date once we'd really started to grow.'

Sahar Hashemi, founder of Coffee Republic:

'When we did the business plan, we calculated we needed £90,000 so we went to the banks to try and get bank loans. We got 19 face-to-face rejections. But it was the 20th bank that somehow believed in us.'

Get selling

Even before you meet with your potential funders, you need to start selling. They'll be really impressed that you already have this most important part of the business under way.

They know that the only reason a business exists is to serve its customers and to earn a profit as a result. Without customers there is no business. The more evidence you can prove of having sales or being near to having your first sales, the more likely they will be to provide you with the funding you require.

If you're going to be operating a B2C business (especially any business where the customer comes to your premises to buy – so this includes restaurants, hairdressers etc. as well as normal shops), then you need to plan your opening day. Use this event to attract as much attention as possible and get as many people as you can to visit your premises. How can you do this?

- Arrange a launch party for invited guests.

- Produce flyers that you can get friends to hand out around the area on the day.

- Distribute vouchers for special offers.

What other ideas can you think of?

If you'll be a B2B company, then you should already have a list of potential customers you want to target in your business plan. Ideally you'll have already persuaded one or more of these people to support your venture and try you out. If not, then now's the time to start talking to them. You need to be doing the following:

- Research them and their industry. Know the challenges they face and what they are aiming for.

- Call them. Ask if it's a convenient moment to talk. If it's not, arrange a time to call back. If it is, then tell them briefly about your new business and ask them about their needs for your type of service. Get to know as much as you can about their needs, their current suppliers, and ask them whether they would be prepared to give you the chance to show that you can help them better than anybody else.

- Send them some more information about your business and your services.

You'll follow this up next week.

Press coverage

Whatever your type of business, it's well worth spending some time preparing to get publicity for your launch in your local or trade media. Often something as simple as a personal letter to the editor or a journalist can get you some coverage if your story is interesting enough. You have to think what will interest other people – the general public – about your business. You may also be able to link it to something else that's currently in the news – local news organisations love being able to get a local angle on a national story.

Things that will interest other people about your business:

- A personal story.

- Something unusual and, even better, amusing.

- Something connected with someone famous, or a major international brand name.

- Something cool and trendy.

Draft a letter or a press release now, ready to send out once you've got your funding confirmed – because you'll be very busy then!

You can get some help on writing press releases and dealing with the media in general from the book recommended on p.179.

Emma

Emma decides to draft a press release that ties the launch of Racing Greens into some research that has just been published showing how different foods affect your alertness and productivity.

22 Week Twenty-Two: Start Selling

This week you'll begin marketing and selling your products and services, and planning your weekly cash flow.

Time to reflect

But first, it's now time to sit back and think, after the hectic pace of the last few months.

Have a look at the pinboard on which you assembled pictures and other things to symbolise your dreams in Week Two. Are they still your dreams or is there anything you want to add, change or take away?

Do you think that running your own business can help you to achieve those dreams?

Have you enjoyed the work of the last few months? Have you found it invigorating to put in all that effort and know that it's your ideas and your energy that will make it work?

Some of you may be a bit scared at this point, particularly if you've decided you need to resign from your current job with a big 'safe and steady' company when you officially start your business – which is now only a few weeks away. That's OK, it's perfectly natural to feel like that, but before you move on you have to be really sure that you'll have no regrets.

Perhaps you'd regret leaving your current 'safe and steady' job if it were like this:

- You have the best boss in the world who listens to all your ideas and regularly thanks you for your work.

- You have a role that allows you to try lots of new and exciting things. If you have an idea, you can just put it into action straight away without seeking permission and writing lots of paperwork, holding lots of meetings etc.

- No stupid rules that drive you up the wall.

- No constant threat of budget cuts or redundancy.

- No management speeches about how 'it's been a good year but we all have to work much harder next year'.

- No great 'new' initiatives, which were actually something you all used to do but were stopped a few years ago as part of a previous 'new' initiative.

- You're so valued there that all the staff would cry if you left, the share price of the company would plummet and customers would be ringing the chief executive, who would then be on the phone within minutes offering you a multi-million pound deal to come back.

If your job is just like this, then perhaps you should re-think your decision to leave.

Seriously though, this is a life-changing decision on the scale of buying a house or starting a family. Make sure that you, your business partner(s) and your husbands, wives, girlfriends or boyfriends are ready for this and excited about the future. Take a few evenings to talk it over.

Funding

It's time to follow up by calling all the people you sent your business plan to. Arrange a meeting with them to answer their questions and get their decision. Ideally this should be next week, but some people won't be able to meet you for a few weeks. It doesn't matter what order you meet people in – often won't give you a decision straight away and, if they do, you don't have to accept straight away. We'll cover how to handle these meetings next week.

Tony Thomson, founder of York Brewery:

'We did presentations to about 8 banks, they all said "wonderful presentation but you can't have any money", until the 8th one who said "we'll support you, up to a point". The cash flow in the early days was on a knife-edge and in the end we had to double the debt to the bank and they went along with us and were very supportive, bless them. But there was a limit to it and we had to be extremely careful not to exceed it.'

THIS WEEK'S TO DO LIST

- ☐ Meet bank managers and decide on a shortlist to negotiate with.
- ☐ Meet accountants and choose one.
- ☐ Meet lawyers and choose one.
- ☐ Decide on the company structure you'll adopt.
- ☐ Decide whether to register for VAT.
- ☐ Remember to keep updating your weekly blog at **www.weekbyweek.net/startyourbusiness**.

LIST OF CONTACTS

Companies House: **www.companieshouse.gov.uk**

They offer a range of useful guides about what's involved in starting a limited company and what your legal responsibilities are.

York Place Company Services: **www.yorkplace.co.uk**

They offer a download of a useful, clear booklet called *The Basics of the Limited Company*.

GLOSSARY

VAT: Value Added Tax is a tax that you collect from your customers for Her Majesty's Revenue and Customs (HMRC) by adding (usually) 20 per cent to the prices you sell to your customers at. You then pay this money to HMRC at the end of each quarter. You're also charged this tax by your suppliers on any purchases that you make from them, but you can claim these payments back from HMRC by subtracting them from the amount you're due to pay on your sales. Therefore you're effectively only paying the tax on the difference between the price you sell at and the price you buy at – or the added value that you give to the product between buying the raw materials and selling the finished goods. That's why it's called Value Added Tax. In other countries it's called Sales Tax.

Plan your weekly cash flow

Cash is the food that keeps your business alive. Your new company will eat this food at a surprising pace and your job is to keep finding more food to keep it alive. If you've planned well, you should have a well-stocked larder of cash in the bank, but you'll need to keep restocking this well before you run out. One week without enough cash and your business will be ill, and longer periods could bring it an early and painful death.

Where will this 'food' come from? The best place is customers. This cash becomes yours in return for your services. The other sources of cash cost you money – the bank, other lenders and even your investors cost you money in the long run, as they'll want to be paid back more than they put in. So focus on selling as much as you can, for as good a price as you can get, and getting paid as early as you can. Getting cash from customers is the prime way to feed your business.

If this cash doesn't give your business enough 'food' to survive, then you need to put your business on a planned diet and reduce the amount of money the company eats.

What eats money in your business? Your suppliers, your overheads – and if there's enough after all that – your salary. Keep costs to an absolute minimum and arrange to pay as late as you can. Question every cost. Do you really need it? Can you get it cheaper? Can you get it at a later date? Can you borrow it? Can you get it second-hand?

Because the flow of cash is so important, you need to plan it on a weekly basis for your own records, rather than just the monthly basis that's in your plan.

Use the template on p.180 to develop your own weekly cash flow. At first, plan eight weeks ahead, then, as each week passes, add a new week to the end, as well as updating the existing weeks with the latest information.

You can also use one of the online accounting tools I recommended in Week Fifteen.

Shared Experiences

Geoff Windas FCCA advises many entrepreneurs on how to grow their business:

'Cash for the vast majority of start-ups is a scarce resource and requires careful planning, particularly in the short term. As well as the longer-term cash flow forecast by month, as required by your bank as part of your business plan, you need something to give you much greater day by day control. This can be achieved with a simple rolling weekly forecast of cash in-flows and out-flows for the next two months. Remember, the biggest cause of company failures is running out of cash!'

Simon Woodroffe, founder of YO! Sushi:

'I think there is only one secret to running a very, very, very successful company – don't run out of cash.'

THIS WEEK'S TO DO LIST

- ☐ Arrange meetings with the people you sent your business plan to.
- ☐ Get selling!
- ☐ Plan your publicity.
- ☐ Plan your weekly cash flow.

THIS WEEK'S RECOMMENDED READING

Press Here! Managing the Media for Free Publicity, by Annie Gurton (Pearson).

Your company is registered with Companies House, and there will be occasions on which you will have to submit other forms, for example:

- Appointment or resignation of director(s) or company secretary.

- Granting of a debenture or mortgage on the company's assets (for example, as security on a loan or overdraft). The lender will usually provide you with a form to be submitted.

- On the anniversary of the formation of the company each year, you'll need to submit an Annual Return. This just confirms the address of the company and details of the directors and shareholders. You'll normally receive one from Companies House that's already filled out and you just fill in any changes. It's a very simple form.

- Your annual accounts. Your accountant will prepare these for you. You're unlikely to need to have these audited in the early days, but once you're making sales of more than a few million pounds a year your accountant will tell you that your accounts need to be audited, which adds more expense.

You should give some consideration as to who will take up which official positions in the company:

- Director. This carries a lot of legal responsibility. You must ensure that the company abides by the relevant laws and regulations, and trades in a proper way, otherwise you could be personally punished. Each company must have at least one director. You might decide that each of the founding business partners will be a director.

- Company secretary. Don't be fooled by the title into thinking that this job involves doing the typing and making the tea! The company secretary assists the directors in meeting the statutory requirements, such as completing certain forms and keeping the official registers. This person can also be a director at the same time. These days it's not required to have a company secretary in a small business, so in most cases you can skip this appointment and just appoint directors.

Emma

Emma and Alan have decided to form a limited company, with Emma and Alan both as directors.

Keep selling!

Even while you have all these meetings going on, you need to keep selling. Follow up with the customers you spoke to last week. Phone them. Have they received your information? What questions do they have? Could you meet them to find out more about their business and answer their questions?

As well as following up on your existing sales leads, you need to start a weekly routine. Every week from this week onwards you need to research a number of potential new customers. Every week from next week you need to contact potential customers to find out about them and offer to send them some information. After that you need to meet with them, and then write a proposal, and then follow up.

Along the way, people are going to say no, or show no interest at all. Lots of people. So you're going to need to start with more potential customers than you need to end up with as actual customers. Possibly five or ten times as many.

Start using the Weekly Sales Sheet on p.187 to plan and monitor your sales activity. Start a new sheet each week, and mark down the names of the companies or people as you complete each stage with them.

Every week you need to identify potential new customers and add them to a target list. Have this target list pinned to your noticeboard, or right at the front of your sales file. Then each week you should pick some of these targets to research.

THIS WEEK'S TO DO LIST

- ☐ Pitch to investors.
- ☐ Form the company.
- ☐ Keep selling!

confidence, selling and a positive outlook. They'll also want to see that you have a thorough knowledge of your industry and your marketplace – and the challenges you're likely to face.

Their decision will be primarily about personal chemistry. If they like you, that's more than half the battle won.

Investors: family and friends

If your family and friends have expressed an interest in investing in your business, you should have a formal meeting with them, just as if they were an investor you'd never met before. Remember, though, that they may not be as experienced in business and investing as other investors, and you should make sure that they are aware of the following:

- They should only invest money that they could live without. If the unexpected happens, they could lose it. They should restrict their investment to what they consider a relatively small amount.

- They will not be able to get their money out for quite some time. How long will depend on the profitability of your business and how much you'll need to continue investing in growth, but it could be at least five years.

- They will not get a return on their investment for even longer and you won't be paying dividends for some time either.

- They should only invest if they promise not to hate you if you lose their money!

- They must understand that it's your business and they are not to interfere. You'll ask them if you want advice.

If they're aware of these considerations and they still want to invest, then congratulations – this is the best possible start to your business.

For each person you meet, get a date from them by when they will have made a decision on lending to, or investing in, your business. Emphasise that you're ready to go and would like a decision next week. However, it may well take longer.

Registering your company

If you've decided to register your business as a limited company, then now's the time to do so. It's a very simple process, particularly as I'd recommend that you use a company formation agent. Your accountant can organise this for you, or you can find your own. I've listed a few in the 'List of Contacts' section on p.186. It should cost you around £120 for everything you need. The paperwork is very straightforward and you can do it online. The form of company you're most likely to need is a Private Company Limited by Shares, but do get advice from your accountant or formation agent.

When you form a company through an agent, these are the steps they're likely to take:

1. They will register the company, with the agent as the sole shareholder, director and secretary (just to make it easy for all the paperwork to be filed to them, but they'll later transfer it all to you). Sometimes they will already have done this step, and provide you with what's known as an 'off the shelf' company.

2. If it's an off the shelf company, they will submit a change of name request to Companies House.

3. They will register to transfer the one share in the company to you, and provide a Duty Paid Stock Transfer form to you (transfers of shares are subject to Stamp Duty, a form of taxation).

4. They will appoint the people you have specified as the director(s) and company secretary.

5. The formation agent will resign as director and company secretary.

6. They will then send you the Certificate of Incorporation (and perhaps a Certificate of Change of Name), the Articles and Memorandum of Association, and the company's Statutory Registers. The registers include the details of the directors and the shareholders. All these are very important documents and should be kept safely.

The company is now yours. You can issue further shares, appoint other directors and so on.

DOCUMENTS

Weekly cash flow template

	Week 1	Week 2	Week 3	Week 4	. . . and so on . . .
Cash in bank at week start (A)					
CASH IN					
Cash received					
Cheques clearing					
Credit card deposits					
Other					
TOTAL CASH IN (B)					
CASH OUT					
Wages					
Expenses					
Rent					
Tax					
National Insurance					
VAT					
Utility bills					
Supplier bills					
Other					
TOTAL CASH OUT (C)					
Cash in bank at week end (D) = (A) + (B) – (C)					
If D is negative, shortfall to be funded by . . .					
Overdraft					
Withheld payments					
Loan from owners					
Other					
TOTAL FUNDING					

23 Week Twenty-Three:
Pitching for Funding

This week you'll come to the last stage in your quest for funding to launch your new venture.

Pitching to potential investors

If your plans for funding your business involve selling shares to investors, then this week you'll need to meet them, present your ideas and deal with their questions. The potential investors could be external people who you don't know, or you may have approached friends and family to get involved.

Investors: external

External investors will typically be people with a background in business, who have been very successful in their own right and are now looking to invest in the next generation of businesspeople. They can earn a bigger return on their investment in a successful business than they can by leaving the money in the bank and often they invest for an element of fun or personal interest too. They realise the risks, but will look to protect against as much risk as possible.

When they meet you, they'll be assessing you very carefully as a person, because you're the most crucial factor in the business. Even if it's the best idea in the world, it will fail if you're not up to the job. They will want to see for themselves if you have the entrepreneurial skills we talked about right back in the early weeks – persistence, negotiation,

THIS WEEK'S RECOMMENDED READING

Pitching Hacks: How to Pitch Startups to Investors, by Venture Hacks (lulu.com).

LIST OF CONTACTS

Company formation agents:

You can do this directly at Companies House – go to the 'Start a Company' section at **www.companieshouse.gov.uk**

Jordans: **www.jordans.co.uk**

Quick Formations: **www.quickformations.com**

Your accountant can also help you form the company.

DOCUMENTS

Weekly Sales Sheet

This is an example, adapt it to your own needs.

This week I . . .

Identified five potential new customers and added them to my target list:

1. _____
2. _____
3. _____
4. _____
5. _____

Researched three potential new customers from the target list:

1. _____
2. _____
3. _____

Contacted three potential new customers from the target list:

1. _____
2. _____
3. _____

Spoke to two potential new customers from the target list and sent them information:

1. _____
2. _____

Arranged a meeting with a potential new customer from the target list:

_____

I had meetings with:

_____

_____

I wrote a proposal for:

_____

I followed up proposals by calling/meeting:

_____

_____

I sold:

_____ to _____

24 Week Twenty-Four:
The Big Leap

This week is a big week for your entrepreneurial dreams – potentially joining the business full time, issuing shares and opening the bank account.

You've probably been awaiting the decisions from your potential funders with great nervousness. But this week you should be able to get an answer from them. Angel investors may want a follow-up meeting or phone call; they might even want to go and visit your prospective premises with you, or try out your product or service in some way. They will be more thorough than anyone else, because of a combination of it being their own money and them not knowing you.

Once you've received everyone's decision, have you got enough funding?

'Yes!'

Hurrah! Get written confirmation, and work with your accountant/lawyer/bank manager to get the money into your hands. Move on to the next section below.

'Nearly, but not quite'

OK, where can you make up the difference from? Ask the bank for a little more? Put in a little more yourself? Approach other angel investors? Or can you save that amount of money in some way by spending less than you planned?

'Not even nearly'

Oh dear, sorry to hear that. Take a serious look at your idea, and if you really still believe in it then try to find alternative sources of funding: soft loans, grants, other angel investors – or try to start up in a much smaller, cheaper way.

Resigning!

If you definitely have the funding you need, and you planned to leave your job at the start of your business, then now's the time to resign. Do it nicely, and part on friendly terms. You might even be able to persuade them to become your first customer!

If you've been unemployed and registered with a Jobcentre, you need to tell them that you're about to start working for yourself.

If you're going to be trading as sole trader or partnership, you need to register as self-employed with HMRC. Alternatively, you need to set yourself up as an employee on your new company's systems and your company will need to register for the PAYE scheme with HMRC. You'll need the P45 from your last job. Your accountant can help you with this.

However, if there's any way you can run your business part time for a while first, before you quit your job, do try that.

Emma

Emma and Alan meet up before work for a coffee and a confidence boost, then go and hand in their resignations. Emma's boss is sorry that she's leaving, but thinks her business idea is brilliant and promises to get his lunch from there. Alan's boss thinks he's crazy and tries to talk him out of it, explaining about the pension he'll be giving up and the job security he'll be leaving behind. At the end of the day they meet Emma's boyfriend and Alan's girlfriend in town for some serious drinking and a nice meal to celebrate this landmark.

Start getting your other resources in place

You can now firm up your arrangements on renting premises, buying your first stock and buying all the other resources you need. You'll need to do a lot of work on this over the next couple of weeks as well as doing everything else! It's worth doing a big To Do list that you can tick off as you go.

Keep selling!

Remember that your main focus at the moment is on getting your first sales, so keep working through your weekly sales sheet, researching new potential customers, calling people, writing proposals and having meetings. You'll be getting your first few 'Noes' by now, but that means you're getting closer to your first 'Yes'. This is particularly true of B2B selling.

Emma has persuaded a local women's networking club to let her provide the catering and do a short talk in the week that Racing Greens will open. It's an evening event, but at least it won't clash with the busy time in the shop!

Opening the bank account

You should have received your company registration documents, in which case it's time to make the final decision of which bank to open your account with.

You'll need to submit your Certificate of Incorporation for your bank manager to see and take a copy of. They may even want to see your Memorandum and Articles of Association.

You'll also need to take along a couple of forms of identification with you for each person in your management team, such as a passport or driving licence, and some kind of bank statement or bill that shows your home address.

If you like, you can arrange a meeting with your bank manager and they will do a lot of the form filling for you. You then just have to sign in the correct place!

Ask them if they can give you details of your account number(s) now so that you can start opening accounts with your suppliers. Your cheque books and paying-in books will take a week or so to arrive.

Issuing shares to investors

If friends, family or outside investors have agreed to buy shares in your company, then now's the time to issue them.

In the pack that you received when you registered your limited company, there will be some blank share certificates. Fill in a share certificate for each investor.

In the Memorandum of Association that you also received, you'll find details of the share capital of your company, telling you what the maximum number of shares that can be issued is and what each share costs. An example is: 'The share capital of the Company is £1,000. This is divided into 1,000 shares of £1 each', but you could have 100 shares of £1,000 or 1,000,000 of 10 pence.

In this case, the value of £1 is the nominal value of each share, and this is the value that should be put on the share certificate. However, you may charge much more than this for a share.

What will matter to your shareholders are the percentages. So if you have agreed that your rich aunt is going to buy 10 per cent of the company for an investment of £5,000, for example, then you would issue nine shares to yourself (and pay £9) and you would issue one share to her (for which she would pay £5,000).

Of her investment, £1 would be the nominal value of the share, and £4,999 would be what's called a share premium. She's betting that in five or ten years she'll be able to sell her 10 per cent of the company for much more than £5,000, so she's willing to pay a premium now for future rewards.

Your accountant will be able to give more detailed advice based on your circumstances.

You may also be able to register your shares under the Enterprise Investment Scheme. This will provide a benefit to your shareholders in this tax year, allowing them to offset some of the investment in your company against tax. This is a very attractive scheme to many professional investors and can help persuade them to invest in your company.

Emma

Emma has decided that their original idea that she should have 80 per cent of the shares and Alan 20 per cent is no longer suitable, as they have both invested money and are both working just as hard in the business and bringing complementary skills. She suggests that Alan should have 40 per cent and she should have 60 per cent, still having some more shares for coming up with the idea. Alan is delighted and accepts. They issue ten shares in total with Emma having six and Alan having four. Emma pays £2 into the company (to pay the nominal price of her two extra shares) and they each invest £2,500 in the company for four shares each.

Keep selling!

Did I mention that it's really important to be focusing on sales at the moment?

Shared Experiences

Zef Eisenburg is the founder of Maximuscle and a former Young Entrepreneur of the Year. He knows the value of lists!

'I'm what you'd probably call an obsessive list writer and I expect everyone in the company to follow that. That's the only thing I really insist on. Everyone has a today list and before they leave every day they have to update the today list to know what phone calls they've got to do, what meetings they've got to attend, who they've got to speak to, what priority things are for the next day because I believe that unless you're focused in your job and you're organised in every area, you're going to end up drifting as opposed to achieving goals.'

THIS WEEK'S TO DO LIST

☐ Review the feedback from funders and take any steps necessary to seek more funding.

☐ Resign from your day job if necessary.

☐ Write a big To Do list of everything you need to get done in order to launch.

☐ Open the bank account.

☐ Issue shares to investors if necessary.

☐ Keep at it with your weekly sales routine.

25 Week Twenty-Five:

Making it Official

This week you're going to do all the final official paperwork you need to do in order to open your business.

Opening supplier accounts

You'll have to complete a form to open an account with each of your suppliers. They'll want to know the company name, registered number, address, details of directors, your bank details and how much credit you expect to need from them. The forms will be one or two pages of A4, and each supplier will provide you with their own.

By signing the form you'll be agreeing to the supplier's terms and conditions of sale, so ask to see these too if they aren't included as part of the form.

Some suppliers will offer you credit only after you have paid for your first order in advance.

Registering with HMRC

If you're not already registered with HMRC as the result of any earlier enquiries with them, then you should register now. I do recommend asking for a meeting with someone from their Business Support Team, or going to one of their workshops. They really do try to be very helpful.

Your accountant will also be able to advise you on all matters relating to HMRC and may even do the registration for you if you ask nicely!

If you're going to register for VAT, then take some time to read through the other leaflets that you ordered from HMRC. Consider:

- Do you want to register under the flat-rate scheme for small businesses?

- Do you want to account for VAT under the cash accounting scheme?

- Is there a special retail scheme for you?

- Do you want to register under the annual accounting scheme?

Your accountant can also help you make these decisions. I also highly recommend talking it over with the advisers at HMRC. They're extremely helpful, and really will give you advice that is genuinely the best for you – not just for them getting the most tax. You can call their VAT, Excise and Customs helpline on 0845 010 9000.

HMRC will want the following payments from you:

- **National Insurance**. These are payments that entitle you and any employees to receive benefits and healthcare.

- **Income Tax**. If you're a sole trader or partnership, you'll have to pay Income Tax through the Self-Assessment scheme. If you're running a limited company, the company will deduct Income Tax from your salary and pay it to the Inland Revenue – just like the companies you have worked for before.

- **Corporation Tax**. If you're running a limited company, then it will pay Corporation Tax on its profits each year.

- **VAT.** VAT will be payable, if you decided to register for it.

Who else do you need to register with?

Your accountant and lawyer can help you here if you ask them the question, but here's some guidance:

Valuation Office

You may need to register to pay Business Rates on your premises. Visit **www.voa.gov.uk** to find out. You can get the details of your local office from this website, or check your rateable value online.

Health and Safety Executive

You may need to register with the Health and Safety Executive (HSE), particularly if you're employing people or members of the public will be visiting your premises. You can find out more at **www.hse.gov.uk** or by calling its Infoline on 08701 545500.

Local authority/magistrate's court

You may need to obtain a licence from your local authority (council) or your local magistrate's court if you run certain types of businesses, including pubs, hotels, B&Bs, cinemas, nightclubs, sports venues, acupuncture or massage clinics and hairdressers. You'll find details of your council in your phone book, or ask at your local library or Business Link.

Data protection

It's now more than likely that you'll need to register with the Data Protection Registrar, telling them what information you're going to store about people and how you'll use it. You may have customer records, employee records or other databases or files – and even your CCTV security system needs to be registered. Registration is fairly straightforward though.

Office of Fair Trading (OFT)

If you'll be providing credit facilities to consumers, you will need to register with the OFT.

Fire service

Previously you would have needed a fire certificate for your premises, particularly if you'll be providing accommodation to the public (such as a hotel or guesthouse), if the public will be visiting your premises (such as a shop or restaurant), or if there'll be more than one business operating from your premises. The law is about to change and you'll no longer need a certificate, but you will have to show that you've put adequate precautions in place to prevent against fire. Ask your Health and Safety Executive contact or your local Business Link for advice.

Food Standards Agency/Environmental Health

If you'll be making, handling or selling food, you'll need to comply with regulations set down by the Food Standards Agency and register with your local authority's Environmental Health Department. Look up your local Environmental Health Department in the phone book, at your local library or ask your Business Link.

Disability Rights Commission

If your business is providing services to the general public, then the regulations require you not to discriminate against disabled people. You must make 'reasonable' adjustments to your premises or services to allow disabled people to access them.

Other agencies

Ask your local Business Link for advice on your particular business, as there may be specialist regulations or agencies that you need to work with.

Keep selling!

This is the most important thing on your To Do list. Keep at it!

Emma

This week Emma and Alan sign the lease on their shop and are given the keys. They work hard each evening, cleaning and redecorating it. They've had a sign made and fitted, which looks very smart and features a 1920s-style racing car in the British racing green colour, being driven by a tomato wearing goggles! Emma went shopping last weekend and has got lots of old pictures of racing cars from the 1920s and model racing cars in British racing green. They'll use these to add some character to the shop.

During their lunch hours they've been handing out leaflets promoting their 'preview' offer next week and they deliver some of these leaflets to the big employers in the area, persuading people to put them on noticeboards. Emma sends off her press release to the local news media and gets a call from the local BBC radio station who want to come to the shop on Monday morning to interview her about the backlash against traditional fast food and the rise in health-conscious snacks.

The first delivery of fruit, vegetables and the other food they need is set to arrive on Monday morning at 8 a.m. The counter, display chillers, fridges and other equipment are delivered during the week, and by Friday – the last day in their old jobs for both of them – the place is looking great. They're supposed to go out drinking on Friday night, but instead end up taking their partners, bottles of champagne and a big bag of food to the shop where Emma works her magic and prepares a feast. They eat it sitting on the floor. They can't quite believe what they've achieved already, or that they'll open for business (their 'preview' week) on Monday!

THIS WEEK'S TO DO LIST

- ☐ Open supplier accounts.
- ☐ Register with HMRC.
- ☐ Check if you need to register with anyone else.
- ☐ Check what regulations you need to comply with.

▶

- [ ] Work through the launch checklist you prepared last week until everything is ticked off.
- [ ] Sell and promote your products and business.
- [ ] Keep up with your weekly sales routine.

THIS WEEK'S RECOMMENDED READING

A Book About Innocent: Our Story and Some Things We've Learned, by Innocent (Michael Joseph).

Take some inspiration from the story of these three friends who founded a highly successful fruit drinks company.

LIST OF CONTACTS

Data Protection Register: **www.dataprotection.gov.uk**

Disability Rights Commission: **www.drc-gb.org**

Food Standards Agency: **www.food.gov.uk**

HMRC: **www.hmrc.gov.uk**

HSE: **www.hse.gov.uk**

Magistrate's Courts: **www.courtservice.gov.uk**

Office of Fair Trading: **www.oft.gov.uk**

Valuation Office: **www.voa.gov.uk**

26 Week Twenty-Six: Launch!

This week you'll launch your new business after six months of hard work, welcoming your first customers and making money for the first time.

The time has finally come. After all these weeks of building your dream, you've made it. Your business is about to launch.

Launching a business serving the public

If you're running a shop, restaurant or other business, get ready for the general public! The key thing is to make sure that you have the following ready for your opening:

- A float – the cash to give change to your customers. If you have lots of prices that end in 99p you'll need a lot of 1p pieces; you'll also need to be able to give change from a £20 note.

- All the things you need to process credit cards, if applicable, and make sure you know how to use them!

- A way of giving receipts to your customers – either from a till or you'll need to get a carbon-copy receipt book from a stationers.

- Some leaflets to give to each customer so that they have something to remind them of you and some details of all your other products. They can also pass these on to other people.

The impression you make on your early customers is very important. If you can give them great service, they'll tell as many people as they can – people love to be seen to be the first to know about exciting new things!

You can build on this using these ideas:

- In the first week or month, give each customer some vouchers for a special offer that they can pass on to their friend or use themselves on a repeat visit. The best offer from your point of view is giving them something extra rather than giving them a pure cash discount.

- For some retail businesses, particularly restaurants/cafés etc., it can bring huge rewards if you do some special preview events for taxi drivers, hairdressers and guest house owners. Lay on the red carpet treatment for them and they'll tell everybody (at length)!

- Are there local groups or networks who you could tap into? The WI, Round Table, Chamber of Commerce etc.? Perhaps you could do an offer or an event for their members? If what you do is interesting or unusual, then they're always looking for people to speak at their events.

Launching a business serving other businesses

If you're selling to other companies, your hard sales work of the last few months should be paying off. You'll have had a lot of people say 'No', but hopefully you'll now have had a 'Yes'.

Make sure that the terms of the deal are very clear. It may even be wise to draw up a contract, particularly if you're dealing with large sums of money or a long period of time, but in the short term, while you test your idea, you may be able to make do with writing to the client confirming everything that you have agreed. Once your business idea has been proved, it's then worth investing in a lawyer to write some standard 'terms and conditions of sale' for all your clients, or to develop a template contract so that you can fill in the gaps for each client.

You'll want to invoice your client though! This is how you request payment from them. An example invoice is shown on p.206. The key details to have on an invoice are:

- Your company name, address and telephone number.

- The date and a unique invoice number.

- If you're a limited company, your registered company number and registered address.

- If you're registered for VAT, you must show how much VAT is included in the invoice and your VAT registration number must be shown.

- You'll then list the products or services purchased and how much you're charging for them.

It's a great feeling to send out your first invoice (and it never really fades for later invoices either!). It's a feeling that's only surpassed by having your invoice paid!

Start a ring binder called Sales Invoices, with one subject divider inside. As you create an invoice, put it in the front of this folder. As each invoice is paid, move it behind the subject divider. In each section, keep the invoices in order of their invoice number.

Emma

Despite working hard over the weekend making sure the shop is tidy and welcoming, the menus are written and a host of other little details are sorted out, both Emma and Alan arrive at the shop at 7 a.m. on the Monday morning. They're excited and nervous. The food delivery arrives late at 8.15, and it's the most excruciating 15 minutes of their lives. As soon as it arrives they begin preparing the standard menu salads to go on display, and arranging the ingredients for the pick-your-own salads and juices nicely. This work is only interrupted by the arrival of the radio reporter at 8.30 and, at 8.42, Emma – shaking like a leaf – goes live on the airwaves across the city.

When the shop opens at 11.30, they wait expectantly for their first customer. They wait, and wait. The tension rises and they hardly say a word to each other from 11.45 onwards. But at 12.15 Emma's old boss walks into the shop with one of her former colleagues. They've come to buy lunch for the whole team – that's twelve salads sold. They have their first customer.

Shared Experiences

Jonathan Elvidge still clearly remembers opening the doors of the very first Gadget Shop in 1991:

'Quarter of an hour before we opened, when a huge queue of people had built up outside this big new shopping centre we were part of, one of the shop staff I'd hired mentioned the word "float", and that you need some money in the till to give change to people. I hadn't thought of this. I'd thought of all sorts of intricate detail but I hadn't thought of something so simple, so I had to run out of the shopping centre to the bank, and got back to the shop just in time to give change to our very first customer.'

Sometimes it can take a while for your business to get going, as Sahar Hashemi, founder of Coffee Republic, found out:

'By the end of March after we opened we were seriously thinking it wouldn't work, because we were only taking £200 of sales a week. But come April, the weather changed, and people started walking around more and more people were coming. At the same time we got a bit of press coverage and it just tipped in our favour.'

THIS WEEK'S TO DO LIST

☐ Win your first sale from your first customer.

☐ Charge them money.

☐ Celebrate!

☐ Update your weekly blog at **www.weekbyweek.net/ startyourbusiness** to announce your launch.

THIS WEEK'S RECOMMENDED READING

Double Your Business, by Lee Duncan (Pearson).

You don't need to get started with reading this straight away, but when you're ready to move your business to the next stage it'll help you make sure everything is in good shape.

DOCUMENTS: INVOICE

Your Company Name or Logo

To: Mr Nice Client
Client Company
Address Street
Address Town
Postcode

Invoice

Invoice Number: 1201   **Invoice Date:** 15th November 2012

Your product/service: 10 units/hours @ £100 per unit/hour	£1000.00
Travel costs	£82.00
Other expenses	£20.00

SUBTOTAL	£1102.00
VAT @ 20%	*£220.40*
TOTAL	**£1322.40**

Terms strictly 30 days net.

Cheques should be made payable to 'Your Company Name <u>Ltd</u>'

Electronic payments should be sent to:
Account Name: Your Company Name <u>Ltd</u>
Bank Name: Bloggs Bank
Sort Code: 00-01-02
Account Number: 012345678

Your Company Name <u>Ltd</u>, Address, Town, Postcode
Telephone: 01234 5667898 Email: yourname@example.com

Proprietor(s): Your Name(s)
<u>Registered in England and Wales No. 1234567</u>
VAT Reg no.: 123 4567 89

NOTES to adapting the sample invoice for your use:
1. UNDERLINED items should only be included if you have registered as a limited company.
2. ITALICISED items should only be included if you have registered for VAT.
3. The line for Proprietor(s) should only be included if you are a sole trader or partnership.
4. You can issue your first invoice with any 'Invoice Number', but all invoices after that should be numbered consecutively.

Keep going

You're now an entrepreneur. You've succeeded in starting your business after six months of very hard work. Congratulations.

So what happens next? You keep on keeping on…

Keep selling

You could have guessed really, couldn't you? This is your number one priority, finding and winning new customers.

Keep your customers

When people try you out, you've overcome the biggest hurdle. If you give them good service, a quality product and perhaps even a little bit of that love we talked about, then you can keep them coming back. Make them happy.

Keep learning

Successful entrepreneurs are always learning new things –new techniques in their industry, new technology, new business ideas, anything that can help make their business more successful tomorrow than it is today. I recommend that you subscribe to magazines, read lots of books, read a newspaper and go to business seminars and events. And keep conducting those experiments to find ways to make your business, and your product or service, even better.

Keep proper records

You need to keep all the invoices and receipts for the expenses you incur, and all the invoices you send out or receipts of cash sales. By law, you need to keep these in good order for at least six years!

At least once a month, do a proper set of accounts on a computer program or paper records.

Keep checking your progress against your plan

At least once a month measure your progress against your original plan. It's very unlikely to be exactly the same as you originally forecast, but it's important to find out what's different and why. What different decisions do you need to make as a result?

Keep your chin up

There'll be tough days, days you question why you ever did this, and days you think about giving up. Everyone has that, and it'll pass. Focus on the positives, solve the problems as best you can and do the work that needs to be done.

Keep in touch

Firstly, keep in touch with the community of other readers of this book, and me, at the website: **www.weekbyweek.net/startyourbusiness**. Keep your blog going with details of your progress and, if you felt that you received a lot of help from others on the site when starting up, then pay it forward – take the time to answer the questions from those who are only just starting out.

Also, do keep in touch with me. I'll be following your progress on your blog, but I always enjoy receiving emails from readers about their adventures in business and reply to as many as I can. You can contact me at **steve@steveparks.co.uk**

Good luck, and have fun!

Steve Parks

Epilogue

Racing Greens

Emma and Alan have never been so exhausted in their lives. They worked solidly last week, taking it in turns to arrive in time for the 8 o'clock delivery, the other one getting to work at 9. Then they prepare all the food and open the shop at 11.30.

They're starting to get their first orders for deliveries, so Alan goes out and delivers those between 10.30 and 12. The shop is then already fairly busy between 12 and 1.30. They close at 2.30, clear up and then deliver leaflets, posters and coupons to local offices. They get back at 5, Alan cashes up and does the admin while Emma works on designing more promotional materials, getting them printed or copied at the local copy shop and working on the menu. They tend to finish at between 8 and 9 o'clock in the evening.

They don't open the shop on Saturdays because the office workers aren't around, but they both ended up working all day Saturday, catching up and reviewing their progress against their business plan.

They've made more sales in their first week than they expected to, because of the success of their leaflet and poster campaign, but they hadn't anticipated the cost of the promotional event that Emma is doing this week for the businesswomen's networking club. She's decided to really go to town and lay on a luxury feast, but Alan's worried about the cost.

Emma persuades him that if she can convert these people into fans of Racing Greens, they'll not only become regular customers but they'll tell everyone they know. The event is a huge success and Emma, ever the saleswoman, doesn't let anyone leave until she's taken their delivery order for lunch the next day.

At the end of their second week of business Emma and Alan are so excited about the prospects for the future. They're already thinking of taking on their first member of staff. They've had great feedback from their customers and lots of repeat business.

It all started with a dream that Emma had six months ago. Through creativity, persistence and plain hard work she, along with her business partner Alan, has made it happen. She's an entrepreneur and she's never felt so free, and so fulfilled, in her life. But this is just the start…

Index